Adults Molested as Children: A Survivor's Manual for Women & Men

Euan Bear
with
Peter T. Dimock, ACSW

Preface: Linda Tschirhart Sanford, LICSW

Safer Society Press
Shoreham Depot Road
RR #1, Box 24-B
Orwell, VT 05760-9756

Design: Theresa McCloud
Cover Graphic: Delores Pomplas
Illustrations: Michaela Rowan

Editors: Euan Bear and Fay Honey Knopp

Order from:
Safer Society Press
Shoreham Depot Road
Orwell, Vermont 05760
(802) 897-7541

single copy $12.95
10-24 copies $10.00
25 or more copies . . . .$ 9.00

Single-copy price includes postage & handling, prepaid
Vermont residents please add sales tax

This book is dedicated to all the women and men who survived a childhood of sexual abuse—those who became strong enough to write and speak about their experiences and those who have not yet found their voices. It is written in memory of all the children who did not survive, whose lives were taken from them early or who took their own lives later to escape pain and injustice. It is dedicated to a future in which books like this will no longer be needed because all children will be cherished and not abused. It is written for the hope, love, joy, and life we all deserve.

Acknowledgments: We appreciate the comments and support of Lauren Berrizbeitia, Judy Breitmeyer, Don Cotton, Anne-Marie Eriksson, Erik A. Eriksson, Carol Bernstein Ferry, Karen Dashiff Gilovich, Kevin Gregorson, Burton Knopp, Lois B. Lackey, Faith Lowell, Robin Mide, Jo Schneiderman, Ken Singer, William F. Stevenson, Margaret Stinson, Jim Struve, and Leah Wittenberg.

Contents

Preface

Abuse is something that is done to us. It is not who we are. This, above all else, is the message of *Adults Molested as Children: A Survivor's Manual for Women & Men* and it is a long time in coming. No human being has ever been abused because they provoked it, deserved it, or were put on earth to endure such crimes. Abuse happens because the abuser has a problem. To recover, we must separate our sense of self-worth from the experience of the abuse.

I believe this book can and will help many people to make that separation. One of the most difficult aspects of living with abuse in our pasts can be that gnawing feeling of isolation. "Am I the only person this has ever happened to? Does that mean there was something about me that made it happen?" Even now, with all the media attention to child sexual abuse, we can wonder if anyone else ever experienced the same type or extent of abuse or felt the same way afterward. The authors have gone a long way toward helping us to feel less alone. Specifically as we come to understand that women and men share this experience, we can feel less alone and less different.

So often our thoughts and feelings in the aftermath of the abuse can feel "crazy" or "wrong" or "bad." Sometimes we don't know that we are having a "normal reaction to an abnormal situation." We sometimes lack compassion with ourselves and judge ourselves harshly when our old ways of surviving get us into trouble with people who are *not* like the abusers. It can also be difficult to break the habit of generalizing our experience with an offender to all people or all women or all men. We have stuffed feelings down for a lifetime; when we begin to feel a little, it might seem like a tidal wave compared to what we are used to. Reassurance that we are on the right track helps us know that this is a part of outgrowing the pain.

No matter at what point we happen to be in our process, this manual has something to offer. It can be a good beginning if the reader ventures forth, following some of the suggestions that involve talking with caring people. If the reader has already told the secret, this book can be reassuring and affirming. It can also help people important to us understand some of our past without having to explain every aspect ourselves. And, it is one of the best ways helping professionals can raise their awareness of the experience of the victim or survivor.

Survival is not enough. Together we can move on to the celebration of life that each of us deserves.

Linda Tschirhart Sanford, LICSW
Author, *The Silent Children*
Boston, Massachusetts
February 1988

Introduction

There are many books written by, for and about the victims of child sexual abuse. Most are clinical, or written by therapists and social workers. Others contain detailed accounts of the abuse itself. In this manual we take a slightly different approach.

Our goal is to write from the victim/survivor's perspective not only about the experience of child sexual abuse, but about the process of coming to terms with that experience in everyday life. We write about the abuser with an awareness of the society which contributes to his or her capacity to abuse others. Included in that awareness is the fact that most *known* abusers of both boys and girls are men. We know also that women subject children to sexual abuse.

We write for victims who have no champions in "mainstream" society—adults who were molested in families of Black, Hispanic, Asian, and Indigenous cultures; lesbians; and gay and straight men—whose experiences of abuse continue to be denied and ignored in treatment literature, and exploited for the continuance of racist and homophobic myths in the legal system and in pornography.

Our perspective may also be helpful to survivors who grew up with physical or developmental disabilities, a population at high risk for abuse. There may be more issues involved for this group than we have addressed directly.

This manual is written for both women and men survivors with the recognition that there are similarities and differences in both how the abuse occurs and how victims are affected by it.

Because it wasn't known until recently that a large number of men had been sexually abused as children, this is the first publication we know of that is written to include male survivors. The reason lies in how we as a society teach ourselves to have certain expectations of the way women and men ought to behave. We expect men to be physically strong, emotionally invulnerable and sexually aggressive while we see women as the opposite. While this is changing, these stereotypes have made it difficult to see males as victims and females as molesters. We know now that both women and men abuse and are abused.

While the emergence of male victims of child sexual abuse has recently become an area of special concern to sociologists and therapists, we recognize that the stories and survival strategies of women have paved the way. Women first broke the taboo on speaking of the abuse they endured. Women insisted that Freud and others were wrong, and that these stories were real events, not childhood fantasies. Women learned that talking about their experiences with other survivors could help.

This book is written from within the experience of abuse and the process of survival. It focuses less on specific details of survivors' stories than on the similar effects created by all kinds of abuse. It recognizes with respect the strategies that got us this far. It endorses no single strategy for coping now, but suggests several steps that have been helpful to other survivors.

But most of all, it reminds survivors and those around us that this process is *ours,* that our lives belong to us, and that we have the power to change the world, beginning with ourselves.

Society—as well as the victim/survivors and the people in their immediate circles of support—must begin to understand the experience of sexual abuse. It is a profound violation, not only of the child's body, but of the trust implicit in a caretaking relationship. And it has an equally profound effect on how the adult sees and experiences the world.

It is also important for society to recognize that until it understands the effects of child sexual abuse on adult and juvenile sex offenders, most of whom were victimized as children, the cycle of abuse will not end.

We have searched for new language for the ways that victims learn to survive an intolerable situation, language that supports and validates our experience rather than creating a list of isolating "symptoms" which serve primarily to blame the victim and must be "cured." We envision a society in which child sexual abuse is a rare rather than a commonplace occurrence. We hope and work for the creation of communities in which there is true justice for both victims and offenders.

This booklet is for adults beginning to process their own childhood victimization. It is also intended to help explain some of what the victim/survivors may be going through to the significant support people in their lives—families of origin or of choice, marriage partners or "live-togethers," friends, therapists and social workers—anyone whom the victim/survivor wants to understand her or his process. We believe it will also be useful to others who come into contact with victims of child sexual abuse: police officers, emergency room personnel, rape crisis counselors, battered women's advocates, doctors, lawyers, prosecutors, parole officers, and judges.

1
Who, What, and How

Who Are We, and Who Becomes a Victim?

Look at any playground full of children. It is estimated that more than one in every three girls will be sexually molested by a family member or other adult before she reaches the age of 18. Of the boys on that playground, possibly as many as one out of every four will be molested or abused before he is grown. Look at any audience full of adults, and chances are that one person in each row of nine grew up in a family where some member—father, mother, step-parent or parent's girlfriend or boyfriend, brother, sister, uncle, aunt, cousin, or grandparent—used her or him for sexual gratification. Or maybe it was a teacher, priest, minister, rabbi, or a coach, a babysitter, or friend of the family.

Many of the adults in that audience never told anyone what happened to them as children. Both women and men were warned as children never to tell. Both women and men may not understand that what was done to them was abusive, because they were told that it was "love." Because girl children are taught from early childhood that women's most important task is to gratify men's sexual desires, they may not recognize their experience as abuse. Because our culture encourages men to get experience and power by being sexual with women from their teens on, men who were molested in childhood by women are even less likely to recognize it as abuse.

Often, kids are molested by more than one person, or more than one member of the family. There are a lot of us who grew up feeling strange because of the sexual things that adults or older kids made us do, taught us to do, tricked, bribed, seduced or threatened us into doing. The first thing to know is that whether you were molested when you were two, or twelve, eighteen, or any age between, you are not the only one.

"We" are called incest victims, or incest *survivors,* when the person who used us for sex was a member of the family or a member of the household. We are sometimes called "adults molested as children" whether the person who used us for sex was outside or within the family. In this book, we use the word *survivor* for all adults who got through childhood involving sexual abuse, no matter who the abuser was.

It doesn't seem to matter much what kind of family you were in—child molesting happens in rich families and poor ones, isolated families and sociable ones, country families and city ones. Sociologists have tried to come up with a description of a "typical" incest family, but most of the things on their lists could be applied to most families at least some of the time. Families where the person who acts most in charge drinks a lot or uses drugs are a little more likely to be involved in child sexual abuse because the alcohol and drugs help them pretend that there is nothing wrong about what they are doing.

We are also of nearly every race and culture in this country, including Caucasian, Black, Hispanic, Asian, and Indigenous (a word that some Indians—or Native Americans—prefer to use). Because American "white" society as a whole already treats people from other cultures badly, being abused meant more pressure never to tell about being molested. Telling a teacher or a social worker that we were being molested would only make things worse for our people by confirming racist myths they already believed, myths like these: "Black and Hispanic men need more sex than white men;" "Those Indians don't live civilized like us—this proves it;" "Black and Latino families are used to violence, so molesting and battering don't matter very much;" and "Black and Latina women are very strong, so they don't need or want any help."

Some of us are now gay or lesbian, meaning we love and make love with people of our own sex. Some people think that we must have become gay because we had such bad experiences in being abused by a person of the opposite sex. But some lesbians were abused by women, some gay men by men; other lesbians and gay men were never sexually abused in childhood. It doesn't fit that neatly.

Other social scientists have tried to figure out why any given person was victimized. Was there something about that girl or that boy that made it happen? But there is no easy answer or pattern for that either. Sometimes it is the oldest child, the youngest, the one in the middle. Often it is each of the children one after another until they each get to be "too old." Sometimes it is the plain child, or the prettiest/most handsome. Sometimes it is the healthy one, sometimes the sickly or handicapped one. It could be the popular one or the lonely one. Sexual abuse happens to all kinds of children in all kinds of families. There is no one thing, or combination of things, about you personally that "made" the abuse happen. The abuse is not your fault.

There *are* adults who were abused as kids and were able to talk about it at the time—they had an adult friend or family member who was really on their side to make the abuse stop and to help them with their scary mixed-up feelings. When an abused child gets that kind of help, life may not be so hard afterward.

If you are an adult survivor who is beginning to get help now, try to remember that you survived because you made the best of a situation that you had to tolerate alone. You didn't have some one you could really trust to talk to. If you are male, you also grew up learning that boys had to be "strong," weren't supposed to cry, and were always supposed to take care of their own problems. You did the best you could at the time.

You did not deserve the abuse then, and you do not deserve abuse now. You can overcome the effects of the abuse on your life. You do not have to be powerless any more.

What Do We Mean by "Molesting" and "Incest" and "Child Sexual Abuse"? What Exactly Is Done to Children?

All three of these words mean anything sexual someone asked you to do or made you do with your body or theirs or both that made you feel scared and strange inside—though maybe it sometimes felt nice, too—and that they told you to keep a secret. Or you may not have been told directly to keep it a secret, but you knew somewhere inside that if you told, something bad would happen to you or to someone else you cared about.

That might have meant being asked or ordered to take your clothes off, or to look at pictures of other kids or adults who are naked. Some kids were asked or ordered to sit in a man's lap and rock until his face got red and he started breathing hard, or in a woman's lap sucking her breasts. Maybe you had to touch the older person on the penis or the vulva, or he/she rubbed against you naked, or kissed you with his/her tongue, or put his or her fingers or other things inside your vagina or your anus. Some adults have told of being given enemas over and over again in a way that felt like sex and power were involved. Others were never allowed privacy in their bedrooms or bathrooms, and were touched sexually—or "diddled," as one man said—in the bathtub or while dressing. Sometimes the abuse started as something small: Mom or Dad or Uncle Charlie gave you a goodnight kiss and stuck her or his tongue in your mouth or in your ear. Or it was more subtle, like always asking about your period or whether you had a wet dream yet. What makes it abuse is that these things were done not because of concern for you, but only for the adult's pleasure.

Some kids were made by the molesters to have sexual intercourse with them. In some families, the oldest child was treated like an adult lover, no matter how young they actually were. Maybe Mom or Dad slept with you even when you were too old. Or they went on "dates" and ended up telling you about their sexual relationship. From there, it became easy to treat you like a real adult, even sexually.

Some survivors tell of being beaten up before, during, or after the sex, or threatened. Sometimes there was a combination of pain, anger, sex, physical closeness and what felt like "love" or special attention which makes it very confusing for us to sort those things out now that we are adults. In other cases the abuse was brutal and sadistic and was never mixed with affection.

One man we talked to remembered, "My mother would spank us in the nude, and all of us would stand together. My father spanked us by making us place our head between his legs under his 'privates' [while] he spanked us on our rears. . . . I kind of looked forward to that because it was as physically close and intimate as we became."

Those are the most visible "things" that were done to us when we were children, and until now you may not have considered some or all of what was done to you as sexual abuse. While not all of those things were "traumatic," it is important to find out how they affected you then, and how they may still be affecting you now. There were other things going on below the surface that are important to understand, too.

For many of us, it didn't matter to the person who abused us who "we" were. We were just people less powerful that they could use to make themselves feel more powerful, more in control. They used sex to get that feeling of power and control.

But at the same time, some of the molesters gave us money or gifts, attention or privileges that made us feel special. Sometimes, to get those things or to get that special feeling, or to protect other members of the family from harm, we made bargains with the molester. *But we did not start it, nor did we "seduce" the molester.*

There are many books and stories handed down about young girls who torment and tease older men, their fathers or stepfathers, until the men have no choice but to be sexual with the girls. These are fantasies written by men, things they wish would happen so that they do not have to take responsibility for their acts. They are not real, and they have nothing to do with you as a woman survivor.

For young men, the stories are different. They tell of older women "seducing" young boys, and it is all considered part of his "education" in how to be a man. Neither fantasy is ever called what it is: child sexual abuse.

The people who molested us told us lies about what they were doing and why. Because of those lies, many of us feel confused about what happened and about how we felt then. They told us, "this is what people do who love each other." Or "you were bad, now I have to punish you—it's all your fault." Or "you slut, you whore, I'll teach you to screw around with that boy." Or "here, just touch it, I won't ever do anything to hurt you, you can say stop whenever you want." Or "I'm doing this so when you grow up you'll be a good lover, you'll know how to treat your wife." Or "this is our special secret, I wouldn't want your sister's or your friends' feelings hurt, so we won't tell them that I love you more than I love them." The sneakiest and meanest thing about some of these lies is that they made us believe bad things about ourselves that were not true.

No matter how "good" or "bad" your behavior was, it is never all right for an adult to be sexual with a child. It is always the adult's job to set limits, not the child's.

Often the sex started as something else, a kind of play—tickling or wrestling—or a dare, or a joke. When we tried to say "no I don't want to do that," we were punished or humiliated. We wanted what every child wants: affection and love. What we got was used and lied to.

It happens like that between older kids and younger ones who are "friends," and between brothers and sisters, even when they are close in age. A game becomes sex, or you are threatened, ridiculed or made to do weird sexual things in order to feel included. One man talked about how his brother made him get on his hands and knees so a stray dog could hump him while the brother and his friends watched and laughed. A woman recalled how her brother, after abusing her for ten years, held her down so his friends could rape her.

Sometimes the thing that's hardest to understand is how someone who loved us could possibly do something this bad to us. There is a confusion of love and pain that carries over into our adult lives. When someone now says "I love you," we don't know what they mean. Since love back then also meant abuse and powerlessness (obedience), we're not sure we want love now. But love doesn't have to mean pain, and real love doesn't make the loved one powerless. *All survivors deserve love without abuse, just as all other people do.*

How Does Child Sexual Abuse Happen?

We only know parts of the answers to how and why child sexual abuse happens. We know that when a child is sexually abused, it is because someone in the family or close to the family cares more about his or her power, money, and possessions, and about pretending that everything is "normal" (often with the help of alcohol or drugs), than about the well-being of the child. We also know that we in the United States live in a society which cares more about power and possessions than about people's real lives and feelings. It shows in how rich people generally treat poor people, and how badly many white people treat people of other races and cultures. It shows in the way many people treat each other as things, or servants. It shows in the way that many adults go after the power and possessions through driving themselves to work long hours, sometimes neglecting their own emotional and physical needs and the needs of people close to them. When ownership of things confers power, and when adults regard children as power-enhancing things to be owned, the result is abuse.

All children want and need love, touch, and approval to survive, as much as they need food and clothing. Children are small and don't know about the world until they are taught. They depend on parents and other adults to teach them in ways that are not harmful. But molesters, whether in the family or outside of it, take advantage of children's needs for love and approval, and exploit those needs. These adults and older kids use persuasion, bribery, threats, tricks, lies, and violence to make children do what they want, not what is good for the child.

These methods work because most children are insecure, or not sure that they are good "enough." Children learn early that in most conflicts with an adult, they are usually "wrong;" and even when they're right, they may be told they're "bad" for contradicting the adult. It becomes natural for a child to believe that she or he is somehow "bad" rather than that parents or other trusted adults are wrong or unfair. These methods work to keep molesting a secret because children feel ashamed or guilty that they could not stop the molester, or because they are afraid of the reactions of their friends and families. Sometimes they work because there isn't anyone the child could trust to tell about it, or because the child is treated as if she or he is crazy, or lying, or making up stories. Other times, the child is told that her or his silence is protecting members of the family from something terrible, like splitting up, jail, or death.

Sometimes a boy will not tell and cannot escape because he thinks being molested by a man means that he is a homosexual, and he can see and hear that homosexuals are treated badly in our society. Men who were victims also say they could not tell or escape because they knew men—even "baby" men—are supposed to be able to take care of every problem by themselves, without help, and not be scared, and never admit they were victims.

Men who were molested as boys by women may not tell because our male culture doesn't consider that abuse—it is the subject of jokes and stories that call it "luck" or "a good education." But it can be just as confusing and abusive as when an older male molests a young girl, and it teaches the future man that it is all right for adults to be sexual with children.

But the strongest part of how incest and molesting happen is a process called "denial." That is where everyone involved pretends to her- or himself as well as to others that the molesting isn't happening or that it is perfectly normal, it just shouldn't be talked about. Sometimes that is the part that makes victims and survivors feel the worst, because then we learn not to trust our own eyes, our own experiences, our own memories of what happened. Because of denial, some of us have no memories at all.

According to reported information to date, men—especially those who were molested as children—are more likely to be molesters than women. Some women, however, do molest their children or other children entrusted to their care. Some molesters report being victims in their own childhood, but not all. But most adults who were victims do not become molesters. Those who do, may use children for sex because that is what they learned. Some people marry or have relationships and friendships with molesters because unconsciously, that's what feels familiar.

We cannot excuse molesters from responsibility even when they grew up as

victims. Once they are aware, parents who refuse to believe and protect their children from molesters in the family or neighborhood also share in the responsibility for the abuse continuing. Each person is responsible for his or her own choices. Each person decides consciously or unconsciously that his or her own feelings of power or fear of loneliness matter more than what is good for the child. *Every molester should be held responsible for his or her acts.*

If the kind of abuse that was done to you is not in this book, that doesn't mean that it was not sexual abuse. It only means that everyone's story is different, and it would take a bigger book to name all the kinds of abuse and all the kinds of abusers. But there are some things that all of us share in how we dealt with the abuse then and how we are coping with it now.

2
Coping Then and Now

If you are a survivor, chances are you either feel bad or angry a lot of the time, or you do not feel much of anything. Both ways of coping might have pushed you to talk to someone, a therapist or a friend. But as you start to remember and sift through your memories, it is important to look at the ways you acted then, and the ways you act now—even when they do not always work any more—as the things that allowed you to get this far. Some of them may seem pretty "bad," or "sick," from society's point of view. But whatever they were and are, these things helped you to survive.

None of them mean that *you* are "sick" or "bad." You showed resourcefulness and courage in figuring out how to keep going in a crazy situation. You may not feel strong, but you are. Most of us don't recognize our strength, especially when we begin processing the abuse. The feelings seem so overwhelming that we think about—or may even try—committing suicide. But being dead is not what we really want—we only want the pain to stop. It will, though it takes time.

Some of the ways you may have learned to cope are "good" from society's point of view, but you may want to have a more conscious choice about still using those tools in your life.

Some of the ways we survived then are ways we are still using now. Some we may want to change, some we may want to keep. You may have been "treated" or punished for any of them, without ever having talked about why these coping strategies existed in the first place.

Coping Then

Fight

The survivors we have talked to fought back in a lot of creative ways. Some kids were labelled "incorrigible" or uncontrollable, and handed over to the state, where they were treated like delinquents or criminals. Some "acted out" by skipping school, shoplifting, or fighting at school or at home. Others tried to get control in their lives, to set limits, by using food as a protest—refusing to eat, eating only certain foods.

Boys who were abused were more likely to be labelled "trouble-makers," acting tough. Some began to abuse others by beating people up, coercing sex, or hurting or torturing animals.

Some of us fought back in other ways: by seeking out lots of sexual experiences as a way of being tough and striking out against the values the family *said* it had, or as a way of having the power in a sexual situation by being the one to initiate it. Some of us took revenge on the people who were using us for sex in other ways, by burning Dad's shirt with the iron, for example, or by "accidentally" leaving things in the hallways where Mom could trip over them. Still others of us dreamed our revenge in nighttime dreams or in waking fantasies. And some of us fought back by showing on our bodies the pain we felt inside: by cutting ourselves, or burning ourselves with candles and cigarettes, or being "accident-prone."

Others of us fought back in ways that were much less visible. We became "super-responsible." That is, we did all the home chores, got good grades in school, and managed to look on the outside like everything was great. But it was a way of both fighting back against the "bad" feeling inside, and of trying to get approval and control over part of life. It was a way of disproving the negative opinions that our families and abusers had of us. Society treats super-responsible kids better than those who "act out" in other ways, but the source is still abuse. We sometimes asked for help from teachers, guidance counselors or therapists, but usually we didn't get it because no one could see anything wrong. We felt invisible.

Flight

By "flight" we mean all the ways we tried to get away from the abuser, our families—when they were involved in the abuse, or when we saw that they wouldn't protect us from an abuser—or the emotional and physical pain of being treated like a "piece of ass," and not as a real person by someone we used to trust.

Some of us ran away from home—once or many times. And we ran from foster homes (where another abuser often took over, a foster parent or another kid). Some of us waited until we could get married as a way out of our parents' houses, and we married as young as we could. Others, both boys and girls, became prostitutes, before or after running away. And some of us ran so far away from the pain of being sexually abused that we ran into death with pills or razor-slashed veins or car-exhaust poisoning. Some of us tried and did not die, but the abuse stopped while we were in the hospital, and we were taken care of for a while. Often that was the first time we saw a therapist, if our parents had money. And often that therapist was just one more person we could not tell, since the abuser might have been the one paying, and the therapist might not believe us, anyway. The "treatment" may have become another way for the abuser to use his or her money to control us.

For others, the flight from pain happened inside our minds. We were threatened with harm or death if we ever told, and some of us lost our ability to tell by losing our voices for days or years. Some of us buried the abuse away from everyday consciousness with a separate personality—we became "multiple personalities." It was a way of protecting the child part of us from the part that was being used by someone from whom we could not get away.

Some of us just got quiet, tried to stay out of everyone's way, and never expressed emotion, because all we could feel was pain, hurt, confusion, and sometimes anger. No one wants to live with those feelings all the time. It was a little better not to have feelings at all.

The hidden hurt within our minds sometimes came out in our bodies in what are now called "stress illnesses:" ulcers, migraine headaches, so-called "phantom" pains in the back and stomach, and starve/binge eating patterns. A lot of us had nightmares, dreams in which we were attacked by monsters. Sometimes the dreams had sex in them, sometimes not.

Many of us learned to distrust everyone, to look always for a hidden reason behind the actions of others. We became what some people call "paranoid"—but what we call hyper-vigilant—always watching to see if someone was out to hurt us. It was not something we made up, it was something we learned from the family member or family "friend" who really *was* out to hurt us to satisfy his or her own need for power. It was the best way we knew to protect ourselves from its happening again. Some of us are still very aware—more so than most other people—of who has power in a room or a group and of how that power is being used.

Numbing

"Numbing" was another way of not feeling the pain of being abused. Sometimes it is not that different from "flight," because what we were fleeing from was the feeling of being "bad." We smothered or denied our feelings, or we walked around in shock. Survivors talk about feeling as if they lived within a shell they could never let anyone enter. That feeling is called "dissociation."

Not only were we separate from our emotional feelings, but also from our physical bodies. Some survivors could not ordinarily feel physical pain. We would burn or cut ourselves to test whether we could feel it. We had to become so hard, so tough on the outside that no pain would reach the inside, where we were already hurting so much.

A lot of us got away from the pain by not remembering at all what was done to us. We locked the memories away deep inside and forgot any particular incident, or whole chunks of our childhood. It is part of the process called "denial," where all the people involved pretend to themselves and others that the abuse isn't happening, no matter what they saw, felt, and heard. We forgot because the abuse never made sense, no one else admitted it, and we couldn't live with the pain and stay sane. Because we forgot, each time the father, brother, mother, teacher, or whoever started "acting strange" again, it was new. We couldn't remember what it was like the last time, so we didn't have the information to help us get out of the situation. Alarm bells might have gone off in our minds, but because we didn't know what they meant, we couldn't pay attention to them. All we knew was that we "felt funny" around that person. Some of us numbed out with alcohol and drugs, anything to get away from feeling worthless and "bad." Some of us were following the example of our parents, who also used alcohol and drugs—some legal, like tranquilizers, others illegal—to numb out, instead of taking responsibility for their actions.

And others of us lost our dreams. We couldn't even let ourselves dream about the bad things that were being done to us. It was too painful, and too dangerous to our own sanity.

Coping Now

You probably recognize some things you did in your childhood to try to keep on going, in spite of the sexual abuse. Some of those things are still the same now. One survivor we know talks about how time has been "frozen" for her since the abuse began. Even now that she is 30, she does the same things to cope with pain and stress as she did when she was 13. Numbing out with food or alcohol or drugs is still the same, or being accident prone, or running away by moving from one town to another, or having multiple personalities. But sometimes the things we do now are not as obvious as the things we did then.

Some men who are victim/survivors say they learned that becoming like the abuser is a way of feeling powerful and in control. They now make others do what they want by making subtle threats, shouting, or making demands.

Other men who are victim/survivors talk about their current jobs as a kind of running away: one is a long-distance truck driver, another is an airline pilot.

When we become parents, we may "run away" by not paying very good attention to our own children's emotional needs. They remind us of what happened when we were their age. We may get "lost" in our own memories of feeling bad and feeling angry, and not be able to take care of ourselves or our children very well, no matter how much we love them.

In our jobs, we may stay busy, look competent, and act industrious, as a way to feel safe, a hedge against our feelings of fear and vulnerability. We continually try to stay in control—of our jobs, of our feelings, and of our memories. We are loyal, courageous, and responsible, which makes us good employees. But we have a hard time recognizing our own humanness. Or we are still acting out anger against authority by breaking rules and being unable to keep a job.

Others of us have forgotten our abuse, but find ourselves trying to save the world. We become social workers, counselors, teachers, political and social activists. And all the time underneath, the person we're really trying to save is the child we were then. Or we give and give and give in relationships without getting back the same kind of focused attention and care.

Some of us sexualize all our close relationships—the only way we learned how to be close with people was to have sex with them. Or every time we find someone we would like to be close to, we get angry. We pick fights and end relationships because all of a sudden, someone is too close, reminding us of when closeness was dangerous. Or we are afraid that if someone gets too close, they will have all the power, just as the abuser did when we were children. Or they will find out about the abuse and know how "bad" we are.

And some of us are in sexually or physically abusive relationships that we do not know how to get out of. We may be battering our partners to try to be in control, to have the upper hand; we may be the victims of battering partners. We may be talked or threatened into having sex when we don't want to because we want to be close and sometimes be taken care of. We believe it when a physically or emotionally abusive partner tells us we are bad, the abuse is our fault, and no one else would want us. *None of these lies is true.*

Others of us are still "super-responsible," trying to be "perfect" in order to get the love and approval we got only through sex when we were children. Or we will only be in relationships where we can have all the control.

Survivors, both women and men, may numb out our pain by staying very busy, isolating ourselves. We—especially we men—hardly ever ask for help, and since our friendships are usually based on activities like clubs or sports there is hardly anyone in our lives that we could ask for help.

The reason you are reading this book right now is that some way of dealing with the world is not working well any more. But right now, try again to remember that *all of these ways of coping have helped you get this far. They are your strengths. You are not bad,* nor are your ways of coping, whether you decide to change them or not.

3
Discovery:
Telling the Secret and
What Happens Now

Telling the Secret

People used to speak of the "incest taboo," meaning that molesting your own children was such a bad thing that no one would ever do it. In practice, the only taboo was *talking* about incest, or talking about being molested by someone outside the family. Most of us didn't even know there was a word for what was happening to us, whether the abuser was a family member or not. And we were always warned to keep the things that were done to us and the name of the doer a secret, often under threats of harm or death for us or other members of our families.

If we did tell, we were called liars or crazy, so we knew we could never tell again, because liars and crazy people are unwanted, unlovable. Some of us who told were kept away from the molester, but then no one would ever talk about it with us. Or we were so frightened by having to talk to police and social workers and lawyers that we could never really talk about our own feelings in a way that didn't make adults treat us like freaks.

"I have this picture in my memory: There I was, about age nine, in a courtroom, having to tell all these *men* what my *father* was doing to my body," recalled a woman survivor.

Keeping that secret has been necessary but harmful. But now it is even more necessary to tell that secret. We need to tell for our own sanity, to help us deal with our pain, and because we realize that our silence only protects the abuser. It is hard to break that silence. We learn it so young, and hold it inside for so long that it feels like giving up a part of ourselves, or like cutting open our deepest feelings and laying them on the table.

And then we wait for the horrified reaction that confirms our worst fears: "I am so bad, this is so bad, nobody will want to be with me, I am going to die." Those are the child's feelings that are still in our minds, still connected to never telling the secret. It is guilt for being sucked into a bad relationship, shame for not being able to stop it, and fear that somehow, it was our fault.

But now you are an adult. You have some power to control your own life. You do not have to die to get through this pain. The abuse is not your fault.

Whom you decide to tell is important, but a little less important than deciding to tell in the first place. The first person you tell may not know how to respond in a way that helps you. Again, that does not mean you are bad or wrong for telling, only that the other person doesn't know what to do. Try again with someone else. We will have more to say about what we want from the important people in our lives (see Chapter 5).

Letter to a Friend*

Dear Friend:

I am writing to thank you for all your patience and understanding and to explain what I'm feeling. I want to tell you how much I need someone to talk to and feel safe to cry with. I've kept this a secret for years and it's such a relief to find someone that I trust enough to tell my nightmares to.

I realize that at first you were shocked by my story. I felt jealous of your background. You probably resented the fact that I was talking to you about something so complex and disgusting. I may have made you feel very inadequate.

At first you didn't say anything and I became suspicious. I thought you were secretly criticizing me and I was terrified. You seemed so powerful after I told you. Please don't ask me questions like, "Why didn't you tell?" "Did you tell him to stop?" "How long did this go on?!" "How could it have felt good?" "He didn't penetrate you?"

Please don't hate me. Don't find me disgusting as I do. Do you think I'm dirty? Do you question whether I'm to blame? Please help me separate the abuse from the abused. Help me hate the experience without hating myself. Teach me to detach. I wish I had your objectivity.

I often need a lot of your time. I am very selfish in our relationship. I do most of the talking. My energy is always zapped. I don't have anything to give you lately. I'm sorry.

Thank you for your honesty. You found the courage to tell me that my abuser was a very sick person. His actions were inhuman. That is really difficult isn't it? It goes against everything we've been taught. Your anger comforted me tremendously. It taught me that my anger is appropriate and that I'm not a bad person for feeling this way. Someone was sorry that this had happened to me! Someone loved my little girl inside me—even before I could!

* © 1986 Survivors of Incest Anonymous (SIA). Reprinted with permission.

As an adult I've done things I am ashamed of. I need to understand and forgive myself. Punishing myself never earned forgiveness anyway. I'm not a crazy monster, am I?

Your compassion seems bittersweet. Strangers, nonfamily members, can empathize with me and give me what I need. Yet, my whole family-of-origin is rejecting me.

Thank you for holding my hand. I will carry you always in my heart where my freedom now resides.

From,
Your Incest Survivor

Whom Can I Tell: Resources

Rape hotlines, women's health centers and battered women's programs usually have information and people knowledgeable about child sexual abuse for women survivors. In some communities there are now men's resource centers that can refer you to groups or programs. Gay Helplines are often sensitive to facilitating referrals for male survivors. There are also a few nationwide victim-assistance groups who may be able to direct you to survivors' groups in your immediate area (see Appendix B).

If you just want to talk to someone who isn't judgmental, and if you don't want to get into therapy or face-to-face conversations, try calling a suicide hotline.

But I Feel So Bad: What Happens Now?

Many survivors feel relieved at first when they tell their stories, when they break the rule of silence. For other survivors, both women and men, telling the secret is more like reporting an event that happened to someone else. The feelings have been buried so long that the words come out empty. When our friend or counselor reacts by saying that we were abused, it surprises us, maybe even scares us. And then later, we feel as if we are going to, or want to, die. Some of us have gotten this far and then tried—or succeeded in—committing suicide. It felt like the only way out of the pain. But it isn't the only way out. And you are still not bad. You did not deserve the abuse then and you do not deserve the pain now. There is a place beyond the pain that you don't have to die to get to. Changing ways of coping means finding a way through the pain, a way to give the child inside us the comfort now that we could not get then.

What Happens Now

Whom Can I Talk to Now That I've Told: More Resources

A therapist is one person you may want to talk to about the abuse if you can afford it, if you have health insurance that pays mental health benefits, or if counselors in your town have what is called a sliding fee scale. Some therapists offer group therapy for survivors for less money than the cost of individual therapy. Therapy, however, may not be the best or only answer at any particular time in your process.

Therapists can be helpful in processing abuse. A therapist can be your ally, believing in you when it may seem that no one else does. The therapist's job is to listen to you tell what you feel and think, to suggest exercises that will help you know what you feel and why, to help you learn what is true about yourself, and to provide a safe place where you can explore past memories and new ways of thinking and acting.

If you are a member of a minority group, consider finding a therapist who shares your culture. If none are available in your town, you'll need to question therapists about their awareness of and respect for cultural and class differences.[1] Differences between cultures in personal space, family roles, and body language can create misunderstandings between therapist and client.

While some survivors come to therapists to deal with other issues in individual therapy and later realize that they were abused as children, many of us begin working in peer support groups organized by survivors just for survivors, independent of the therapy and mental health system. There we learn that we are really not alone, that we can help each other, that we are not "sick," that we have strengths, talents and information to offer as well as receive. We learn how to talk about our abuse, how society helps it happen, and some ways to be angry about it without hurting ourselves. We may get to a place where we want extra help or a different kind of help on a particular issue than the members of a peer group can offer. Then we may try to find a therapist or a therapist-sponsored group.

There are as yet very few peer support groups available for male survivors. Some Parents United chapters have support groups for men which are facilitated by therapists. Your best resource as a male survivor may be a therapist you can trust who has experience in working with male survivors (see Appendices B and C).

Not all counselors and therapists know how to help survivors. Some therapists may treat your report of incest or sexual abuse as if it didn't really happen, but you wanted it to; they believe that you made up a fantasy that has now become real in your mind. Other therapists may have less offensive beliefs about child molesting, but they may also not have much information or experience in helping survivors. A good therapist is willing not only to explore your feelings about what was done to you, but is also willing to accept and believe it was real. Both things are important. It may be hard, but asking about their experience with survivors of child sexual abuse

---

[1] Further information on cultural issues in therapy for abuse is included in Childhelp USA, 1988, *Survivor's Guide*. See Appendix A.

will save you time, energy, money, and prevent you from being betrayed in another trust relationship (see Appendix C).

Finding a good therapist to work with is difficult, especially in the beginning when you feel ashamed and shaky talking about what was done to you. It might be too hard to ask all the questions you need to in order to make sure this therapist can help you. If you don't feel like you can ask, maybe a friend or advocate can make some calls and ask some questions. But you still need to make the choice of therapist. A choice is not final, it's an experiment to see how things go. If it doesn't work out, you can always make another choice.

There are two "diagnoses" that are often used by therapists for survivors. Many survivors have found that "post traumatic stress disorder" (PTSD) describes their experience. Victims of violent crime, survivors of earthquakes or other natural disasters, and soldiers in wartime share this reaction to terrible life events. Nightmares and flashbacks, extreme anger and anxiety, shock, denial, and guilt are some feelings that come under PTSD.

The second diagnosis some therapists may use for survivors is "borderline personality disorder," a label used for people who are angry, hurt themselves, are or have been sexually promiscuous, have unstable relationships, "dissociate," are afraid of being alone, or feel suicidal. While these descriptions are often true of adult survivors of sexual abuse, the "borderline" label does not take the effects of abuse into account. Some survivors and therapists regard the "borderline" label as a misdiagnosis because therapists are taught that "borderlines" almost never get better, and that is not true for adult survivors. Ask the therapist if she or he feels that most survivors have "Borderline Personality Disorder." If the answer is "yes," you may be better off with a different therapist.

There also may be peer support groups especially for incest survivors, or ones that include all adults molested as children, offered by a local mental health clinic or by a therapist. Frequently, these groups are for women survivors, but sometimes there may be a group for male survivors.

You may want help with problems relating to alcohol or legal or illegal drugs such as tranquilizers, marijuana or cocaine. Some drug and alcohol counseling programs talk about sexual abuse, though that is not their main focus. In meetings of peer support groups like Al-Anon/Adult Children of Alcoholics and Alcoholics Anonymous, members often identify themselves in meetings or afterwards as having been molested in childhood and may meet as a special interest section. Most survivor groups led by therapists require that you be sober for a year if alcohol is a problem for you.

All therapists and groups should guarantee your privacy. Anything you say during any meeting or session is kept confidential, except when you identify children who are being abused, or reveal that you have been molesting children. In those cases, therapists are required to report such abuse to child protective services.

Confidentiality about your treatment is for *your* protection, not the therapist's. You can talk to anyone you want to about your own therapy sessions. The exceptions to confidentiality are to prevent the abuse of more children.

Therapists should be especially careful about your physical and emotional boundaries. They should never touch you without your permission, or cajole or persuade you into letting yourself be touched. Even a friendly hug could be intrusive if you don't want to be touched. Never should any therapist ever touch you sexually, make sexual suggestions, or offer to meet you outside the office socially. Any therapist or counselor who tries to be sexual with you should be reported to his or her professional licensing board. Most states license therapists, which means they have a board of their peers who set standards for practice and to whom they are responsible. Your state mental health or human services department can give you information on where and how to report.

Neither should any member of a peer support group come on to you sexually during the life of the group. The issues of power, sex, and approval are already too complicated to bring them into the group.

But I Still Have All These Feelings: What Happens Now?

When we begin to talk about our childhood memories of sexual abuse we go through some of the same feelings now as were happening then. We feel exposed, as if anyone looking at us can tell we were sexually exploited. We have a hard time staying separate from images and sounds in the world around us. The smell of rotting wood, or cigarette smoke on someone's breath, the sound of running water, or a bedroom door closing, the sight of an older man with a young girl, or a babysitter with a child on her lap, even something as everyday as chopping vegetables can bring back a memory so powerful that it is like reliving the experience. The boundaries between the past and the present, or between your own self and the images others have, get confused or disappear.

Although we are adults now, the children we were still exist inside. Children who are sexually abused are taught that their boundaries don't count. We were not allowed to say no to the abuse or to the abuser. When we said no, we were ignored, tricked or beaten. Even our own bodies were not our own.

Even now, we may have a difficult time saying no to other people's needs, whether it's for sex or dinner or borrowing the car. Learning to say no is one of the lessons we learn as we deal with having been abused. And later, when we've learned to say no and mean it, knowing that it counts, we can learn to say *yes* when we mean it, too.

The process of discovering and beginning to deal with childhood sexual abuse is not the same for everyone. There is no line from step A to step B to step C. It seems to be more like a spiral, circling in and out of memories and pain, and in and out of feeling like you can handle the world. Other people compare it to peeling an onion: there are layers to go through, some of which feel the same as the layers before. It is hard to see "progress." As one man said, "Some days the sexual abuse feels very big and like it is the cause of all the pain in my life. Other times it seems very small and I wonder if it even happened."

One lesson we learn is to give ourselves time. Some people say it takes as long to deal with your memories of child sexual abuse as it did for the abuse to happen. That means that if you were abused for six years, you should give yourself that long to deal with it, though it may not take that long.

Survivor men may have a particularly difficult time giving yourselves enough time. Men learn that if something is wrong, you fix it and go on. Taking the time to explore inner feelings and actually show some of them is not only something you're not used to, but embarrassing and painful. You may be tempted to get through with this whole mess before you've really given yourself a chance. Be patient. It's worth the struggle in the end.

Another thing to remember is that *you* are the expert on your situation. You are the one who was there, the one who remembers, or feels that a memory is there—whether the pictures and details come clear or not. Therapists, support group members and friends can help and can offer information and comfort sometimes, but no one has all the answers or the "only" right way to deal with child sexual abuse.

One of the most difficult things about dealing with child sexual abuse is learning to trust our own inner voices. Because of "denial" and forgetting, we don't always trust our own experiences of what is happening to us, especially when someone is telling us something different, or that it is "for your own good."

But there is a part of us that tries to protect us from pain and abuse. If you can hear that voice at all, listen well. Do not do anything you feel you are not ready to handle. Do not let people touch you without your permission. If a situation or relationship with a therapist or anyone else feels pressured or makes you feel sick and empty inside, it may be abusive. You can tell them "stop" or "no" or "that's not okay." If they do not pay attention to these boundaries, and if your inner voice is telling you to get out, then get out if you can. You can decide later whether to try again with a new therapist or group.

Sometimes your inner voice will tell you two different things at the same time—like "stay" and "run away." If you have had a good experience up until now with your therapist or group, you may want to listen to the voice that says "stay" and work it out. Whatever you decide, you haven't failed. You've made a choice to take care of yourself in the best way you know how; you're even learning new ways to take care of yourself. And that's good.

4
Process, Process, Process

"Process" means change, motion, and action. The process of dealing with past child sexual abuse involves recognition, emotion, and integration. In this chapter we describe some of the feelings, decisions, and actions survivors go through in learning to cope with our pasts.

Everyone's process is different. Here we write about several streams of process, but there are many more. The process for survivors who have been institutionalized in group homes, juvenile halls, jails, or mental institutions, for example, may be different from the process for those who begin by going to a peer support group or a therapist.

Women are institutionalized and/or given drugs to contain or dull the hurt and anger they act out in socially unacceptable ways. Sometimes we are institutionalized so that we won't hurt or kill ourselves because of our pain. Being jailed or institutionalized may only confirm our "bad" behavior and our negative images of ourselves while increasing the opportunities for others to abuse us. The drugs may help us function, but they do not help us deal with the past that has brought us to this place.

The process is again different in ways we are still discovering for men who were victimized—different still for men who became abusers and men who did not. Men tend to use mental health services and are put in mental institutions less often than women. But when male former victims "act out" their anger, or start molesting children, they are sometimes jailed. They may or may not get any help for the original abuse or for their adult offense (see Appendix B). Prisons, like mental hospitals, rarely help the former abuse victim—they just increase the opportunities for others to abuse them.

But whatever your process, give yourself *time*. You may need to take a break from dealing with your past child sexual abuse for a week or a month or more—it doesn't all have to be done at once.

"I think when I started, a lot of the emphasis was on getting your feelings out. Feel everything," said one survivor in a workshop for this book. "I'd try to feel everything and then I'd numb out for weeks. . . . I knew that if I took it slowly I didn't numb out. If you're trying to fit yourself to someone else's program you can get crazy."

Feelings and More Feelings

Some of us start with the idea that we have learned to function quite well, thank you, without ever dealing with our hidden childhood feelings. After all, who would voluntarily experience pain, shame, guilt, humiliation, and fear? One woman after a few weeks in a peer support group protested, "It used to be just *words* I said, a story I told, like it happened to someone else. Why do I have to bring back all these feelings now? I hate this."

But, how ever we have learned to function without those feelings, or to prevent them from surfacing, it isn't enough or it isn't working. Either the feelings are leaking out around our barricades, or having few feelings or none keeps us from being close to people with whom we want to be intimate. Otherwise, we would not have told someone else about being a survivor of child sexual abuse, and you wouldn't be reading this book.

The feelings may leak out in ways we do not at first recognize as having anything to do with a past we have locked away. We have anxiety attacks, or feel angry all the time, screaming and yelling at people we love over small things they have done. We get easily confused when other people make conflicting requests or demands on our time and attention. Or we feel depressed over how much we take care of other people, and don't get taken care of in return. Or we just feel "bad" and want to be dead.

The important thing to remember about feelings is that you do not have to *do* anything they seem to tell you to. The parts of us and of our society that rush to do something about feelings are the parts that want them to be over with, that want to "get rid of them," because they are too scary, too messy, too unpredictable. You can just *have* your feelings, explore them, see what is there.

For many survivors, both women and men, having such feelings is a frightening new experience, because so many of us spent time and energy not having feelings or keeping them under control. We have been afraid all our lives—usually with good reason—that we will drown under a flood of anger and hurt if we take even one brick out of the dam holding those emotions back. But the key is to go beyond the immediate feelings because underneath them are the ones we really need to deal with: anger, grief, fear, and hurt. And beneath them may be still others we haven't felt in a very long time: love, joy, curiosity, a sense of ourselves as "good."

The other key to "processing" feelings is to find people and spaces that are safe, that will support and protect you while you are feeling so vulnerable and out of control.

The safe spaces may be physical—your own room, the group meeting place, under a certain tree—or images inside your mind. The most important thing is that you feel safe there. If other people are involved in a physical meeting place, you can ask for things—pillows, closed curtains or open ones—that help make the space safe for you.

You might create a safe place within your mind—a relaxed scene by a pond, or a picture of Grandma's rocking chair. Picture yourself going to that safe place when you feel scared or overwhelmed by your feelings.

The people—friends, lovers, spouses, peer support group members, therapists—become your "support network." None of them can "fix it," since "fixing it" would mean going back in time and preventing the abuse from happening in the first place. But they can give you information and help in coming to terms with how you want to be in the world. Most importantly, they can just love you and accept you while you go through your feelings.

It is not realistic to think that any member of your support network will always be there when you want him or her to be. They may say no when you really need them, drawing a boundary for themselves. (Learning about boundaries—where they are for other people and how to draw our own—is part of the new information we need to learn.) Try asking a different safe person for help, company or attention when that happens, or try doing something nice for yourself.

Some members of your family may get angry with you for being so emotional, withdrawn, or "nonfunctional." It is all right to ask for—to demand if necessary— and get time to focus just on yourself. While it is important to remember that what is going on in your life affects the people close to you, it is not necessarily your job to meet all their needs.

But most important of all is remembering that no one can be your "savior." Others may help, *but the only person who can really rescue you is you.*

Many of us lost the ability to cry when we had to block our memories and feelings about the abuse at the time it was happening to us. And when we begin working on letting our feelings out, we are afraid that if we start to cry, we will never stop. Others of us feel "lost" or as if we are "falling down a well."

It helps to cry. We have a lot to cry about. Our childhoods were stolen from us by people whom we trusted and who chose to impose their sexuality on us without ever thinking about how it might hurt us. Our tears are about anger, lost childhoods, and betrayal.

That child is still inside you, waiting to be loved and taken care of. Only now, it is up to you to take care of your own child self. And instead of locking her or him in a closet in your mind because your child self is so needy and cries all the time, you can be the caring person you should have had then. All survivors can learn to nurture their own child selves. This may be especially difficult for male survivors, since men are rarely encouraged to be nurturing.

The child's first need is to express feelings. We also need to learn new information about ourselves and about abusers. Learning often starts to happen when the pressure from feelings is released. Then again, sometimes new information—that you are not to blame, not responsible, and not alone—unlocks the door to those feelings.

But even with new information and a new mental understanding, we—especially men—may *think* we're finished, when we haven't really let ourselves in on the feelings. Even when we have the feelings, we want an explanation: "Why am I feeling this way?" or "What can I do to stop feeling like this?" It's hard for us to cry. But the understanding we can find in women's or men's support groups can help us give ourselves and each other that permission.

"One thing I remember very strongly is that I had a very hard time getting any feelings at all. In therapy I was directed to be angry, and I ended up crying," said one survivor we talked to. Another said, "One of the hardest things for me to recover was my tears. So, okay, if I'm going to be angry crying, let me do it that way, and I can have my anger and my tears."

However you cry is also okay. You might want to be alone, or you might want to be with a support person. You might want to be held, or not touched at all. You may want something different each time you cry. It is your process, in whatever way it works best for you.

Many of us feel guilty or ashamed for anything we did that might look now like "cooperating" or "enjoying" the sexual abuse. Those feelings interfere with our ability to feel anger toward the person who abused us. Before we can get to that, we need to let ourselves off the hook. It might mean being told over and over again that it was not your fault, you were not responsible, no matter what the abuser told you about "asking for it." Even if you had an erection or an orgasm or initiated any particular sexual incident, it does not mean you willingly participated.

"One time two of my women friends were talking about sex," a woman survivor said. "We were in a car on a four-hour trip, so it wasn't like I could leave. I started to feel really bad listening to them, because all I could think of was my brother. I started getting a migraine headache. But all of a sudden, it hit me like it never had before—it wasn't my fault. I thought, 'Hey, you didn't do this! This was *done to you.* You don't have to feel bad about that.' I remember feeling that my whole body relaxed one notch, and my headache went away."

Anger may be an even tougher emotion than guilt for most people. It can be threatening to your support people, as well as frightening for you. It brings up the fear of loss and of disapproval. Many survivors are characterized as "too angry" by people around them. But you have a right to be angry. Some one hurt you, then lied about it to you and to others.

Some group leaders report that men who were in male-survivor groups showed more anger than did women in separate groups. And men tended to act on their anger more directly. But we also see survivor men reacting in the same ways that many women do—by being depressed and quiet.

For some of us who have a hard time being angry, finding ways to express that anger that will not get us into trouble or hurt others is a difficult job. Some survivors try punching pillows, but that may not work for you. Others write letters to the abuser, but do not mail them. Still others fantasize about taking revenge as an outlet for their anger. One peer support group spent a session at the lakeshore throwing rocks.

Another survivor we know burned a picture of her abuser and buried the ashes. And others have done role plays in supervised groups or in therapy. Survivors have used art and video as tools to express their anger.

A session or two probably will not deplete your anger—it is something you will deal with over and over again. Like grief, sometimes it sneaks up on you without warning. The trick is to be gentle with yourself. A lover, partner, or close friend can sometimes help you realize that the anger you are feeling is about the abuse in the past, and not really about your life right now.

Others of us learned to survive by being angry all the time, or by covering up other, more hurtful feelings with anger. When we learn what the anger is really about, we can learn how to feel what's underneath it and how to direct anger where it really belongs.

Being Overwhelmed

Once the feelings start, sometimes it is hard to stop them. Not only has their pressure built up over the years, but the world contains images that constantly trigger those feelings. Advertising images of little girls dressed in Mommy's clothes might do it, or the now-frequent news stories about new victims of rape, child molesting, or incest. Movies and television shows constantly use images of men victimizing girls and women, or joking about having sex with younger and younger women, supposedly to entertain their audiences with a thrill of fear and power. And jokes and stories about older women "seducing" teenage boys can be found in many movies.

Being overwhelmed frightens survivors of either sex. It may be tempting to control those overwhelming feelings using things that have worked in the past, like alcohol and drugs, anonymous sex, or working overtime. But it's important not to give in and cover up the feelings. There are other things you can do to reduce your feelings of being overwhelmed and at the same time get practice in making real, conscious choices in your life.

You can make decisions, and act to protect yourself. If you feel panicked and out of control, turn the TV off, leave the theater, and call someone you trust just to touch base. She or he can help you remember that the feelings are from the past—

you are in the present—and can give you support for taking action. One survivor, after explaining to her friends, requested that they warn her about any books they shared or movies they had seen containing rape images. She could then decide if she wanted to see the movie or read the book, and wouldn't feel ambushed by the violence.

There are other practical areas where survivors often feel overwhelmed or triggered. Getting medical or dental care can make us feel particularly victimized. When oral sex was involved in the childhood abuse, having a dentist's fingers and instruments in your mouth can be a horrifying reminder. There are basically two ways to cope: find a sympathetic dentist or medical practitioner who always fully informs you about each action or procedure; and always take a support person with you to help keep you grounded in the present and to be your advocate. A sympathetic practitioner will allow or encourage you to bring your support person into the examining room with you unless there are concerns about keeping the area sterile.

Ask for What You Want

We have lived our lives with secret shame. But the shame does not belong to us—it belongs to the people who abused us. When we break the old lessons and learn new ones, we take control of our own lives, feeling less overwhelmed as time goes on. We make more and more choices about how we want to be in the world, then figure out how to get what we want.

Because child sexual abuse taught us that what we want does not matter, we usually have a terrible time first *knowing* what we want, and then actually daring to ask for it. We grew up believing that if we were to get something, we had to bargain for it or offer something—our bodies or our attention—in return. Some of us learned to disguise what we wanted by phrasing the request as if it came from the other person: "Do you want to . . . ?" Others of us ask questions that immediately assume the other wouldn't want to say yes: "I don't suppose you'd . . ."

These kinds of questions are not usually an issue by themselves, but they are clues to what we have learned about ourselves. The people from whom we learned those lessons are abusers—they lied to us about their actions, their motives, and our worth. We can unlearn these false lessons.

Ideally, survivors learn that we must ask for what we want—and maybe we can even get it—at the same time we're learning that our feelings are okay and that we have a right to express them. Being able to ask for a hug or to be left alone while feeling vulnerable helps the process. We learn that we can affect the world.

As we learn to ask for what we want, we also learn that when others say no, they are not necessarily rejecting *us*. They're setting their own limits about what they can and want to do. And unlike when we were children, punishment doesn't necessarily follow just asking.

Another new lesson is to care less about what other people think about us or about our process. That may sound cold. But the molesters' lesson that we are of worth only by the use of our bodies, gave us no sense of self separate from others' opinions and no real reason inside ourselves to say no or yes. In this way we learned to measure our worth by what others thought of us, instead of by what we think of ourselves. One of our hardest new lessons, especially for survivor women (because society says women should always put others' interests before their own), is to put our own interests first. Since men are usually taught to put their own interests first, some male survivors have a harder time connecting with other people than separating from them.

For survivor men, the hardest lesson may be understanding others' feelings as well as our own. And when survivor men were abused by men, even more issues of trust and safety come up, especially in men's survivor support groups. But it is possible to learn these difficult new lessons and change our lives in ways that make us happy to be alive and proud to be who we are.

Process: On Your Own, with Therapists and in Groups

"Group process" means the ways that people interact with each other in a group. But what we are talking about here are questions that come up whether you are processing the past on your own, within a group, or with a therapist.

One thing that a good group or therapist can do to help is to teach us the skills our parents never did: establishing appropriate boundaries, making friends, playing in a healthy way, and identifying different feelings and emotions.

When we talk about therapists, we primarily mean those who use language and listening as their main tools. There are other kinds of therapists who might be helpful in our process of dealing with past abuse. Some use "body-centered" therapies that help us to understand how we can use our bodies in our healing process.

As survivors, one of the things we often need to do is to reclaim our bodies for ourselves, even to get reacquainted with our bodies after years of denying them. You might need to start slowly in getting to know your body. Look at yourself in a mirror, touch yourself, and massage your tense legs and sore feet when you feel you need it.

Basic massage is helpful when you find a masseuse (a woman) or a masseur (a man) with whom you feel comfortable. It can allow you to explore your own boundaries of touch in a situation that doesn't involve a personal relationship, doesn't involve sex, and that does put you in control of what happens.

Children who have been victims of abuse develop protective body patterns in response to the abuse. Like other survival strategies, these patterns may no longer be helpful and may, in fact, be a source of tension and disease. A number of body-centered therapies may be helpful in learning new patterns of movement, new ways of holding your body, and new techniques for relieving the stress that comes with emotional work on abuse issues.

Given survivors' reasonable concerns about physical boundaries, the kinds of body-centered therapies that encourage your own awareness of how you move and how you hold tension are good ones to try. The Feldenkreis method and the Alexander technique,[1] for example, work mostly on awareness rather than attacking muscle tension directly.

There are also deep body work techniques, Rolfing, for example, that may help you feel different and better in your body. Rolfing involves moving the semi-hardened sheaths of the muscles to help you move more freely. People who have been through Rolfing say that it is painful and may feel invasive. It may also feel like too much to deal with on top of the emotional pain of working out the abuse.

There are other mind/body therapies that are now gaining popularity. But as with any therapy, it pays to investigate what's involved before you commit yourself to it.

Whom Should I Tell About Being a Survivor?

Whom you tell is entirely up to you. If you are seeing a therapist or counselor for some other issues and you trust that person, it is important that he or she know. At some point you may want to tell other significant people in your life.

Other than that, there are no "shoulds." Some survivors feel better as more people in their lives know. Others have told all their friends and then regretted it later. They felt that they wanted it private again, especially if some of their friends treated them differently after knowing.

People will react in different ways to your telling about being abused. Some will sympathize, others may be frightened or disgusted, and some may respond with their own histories of abuse. Friends or lovers may be filled with rage at the abuser in a way that feels frightening to you. Some people may press you for details of the abuse. You can ask a trusted friend or therapist to help you plan whom to tell and how to deal with your feelings about telling and their reactions. You could set up a

---

[1] The Feldenkreis method is taught in two parts. The first is usually in a class with an instructor or a tape. The object is to slow down your movement patterns to help you be aware of how the movement occurs, what other body parts are involved, and how it affects your breathing. For example, one exercise might have you lying on the floor and tilting your pelvis just slightly forward. You may notice tension in your shoulders and neck, or that your chin moves, too. Some practitioners may also encourage you to be aware of any feelings, any emotions that come up with a movement. The second part is more "hands-on" work. The object is to create a safe environment. The practitioner may physically support a tense part of the body in order to let you become aware of the tension. Once that safety is reached, the practitioner tries to open the possibility of new patterns of movement.

The Alexander technique is similar, but primarily focuses on the head and neck. The practitioner may use a gentle hands-on approach to gently guide you into new ways of moving.

Both of these therapies are done when you are fully clothed.

time in advance to check in by phone or in person with your trusted person soon after you've told someone new about the abuse.

"Telling" by itself doesn't deal with the issue—it only deals with the secret. The effects of the abuse and of the secret-keeping are still there.

Does the Pain Ever End?

Yes. And no. It is a lot like grief. In the beginning it may hurt so much that all we want to do is be numb and not be reminded of what hurts. But as time goes by, and with help from friends and other support people, it hurts less and less, especially as we find new ways to deal with the hurt. Finally, it becomes a memory and a lesson from the past, but it only rarely has the power to hurt us any more.

Is Childhood Abuse Responsible for Everything Bad in My Life?

No. But a lot of us almost wish that were true, because then, once we had dealt with the abuse, our lives would be totally wonderful.

It is really tempting to dump everything we feel is negative about ourselves and our lives onto the child sexual abuse. From lying to compulsiveness, from suicide attempts to overeating, from sloppiness to being accident prone, any of what society and therapists may call "negative" behaviors (and we call "survival strategies") may be a response to the abuse. But it may not.

First, the abuse is probably not the only bad thing that happened to you, though it usually feels like the worst. Second, we think *any* behavior that has helped you to survive is okay. Some of these behaviors society generally regards as "good." For example, one survivor mentally escaped from the abusive brother and unseeing family by reading books, newspapers, magazines, anything she could get her hands on. As a result, she was a good student in school, so society thought that was "good."

Another survivor feels very "tuned in" to who has power in a group, a club, a class, a job. She feels that is "good," and she doesn't want to change it, though she knows it is something she learned in a bad situation.

What Do I Do About Sex?

Your sexual energy may change drastically as you process your memories and feelings of childhood sexual abuse. Some survivors go from wanting to be sexual as often as possible, to not wanting to be sexual at all. And some come around to wanting to be sexual again, though in a way that is new, freely chosen, and emotionally as well as physically intimate.

Men who were abused may have a different kind of hard time sorting out sex, since in our society, men are expected always to perform sexually, and to use pressure to create sexual opportunities. The power issues involved in the abuse may mean you are unable to "perform." In other words, associating sex now with feeling powerless in the past when you were forced to be sexual can result in difficulty getting or keeping an erection, difficulty with having an orgasm, or a general lack of interest in being sexual. These have been seen traditionally as "unmasculine" problems; you may try to push yourself to perform in spite of the difficulties. This won't change the situation and will only add to your feelings of failure and frustration. This is normal for male survivors; it can change as you work through your feelings about what happened.

The question really is, what do you *want* to do about sex?

For some survivors and their partners the question becomes, "What if I never want to have sex?" Sometimes making love in even the most positive situations can trigger memories that sour the experience and frustrate us and our partners.

Sex meets a lot of different needs, and not only the need for sex itself. All of us need to be touched, to be comforted, to be held, to be reassured about our bodies, to feel loved. Most of us want the emotional pleasure and tension release of having an orgasm.

There are other ways to express love and to meet each other's needs. When you do not want to "have sex" you and your partner can figure out together what other kinds of touching or attention will provide comfort, closeness, reassurance, pleasure, and release.

With a loving and committed partner, it is an issue of trust. Can your partner trust you enough to give you the power over when to have sex? Can you trust yourself enough not to use that power in a manipulative way? *You should always have the power to say no,* to draw that boundary, without being punished for it. *No sex should be coerced.*

At some point you may ("at last," after a time without sex between you and your partner) want to have sex, feeling like you are being very vulnerable in offering this "gift" to your partner. But your partner might not want to have sex at that particular time. Just remember, it is not a rejection of you—your partner has the right to say no, too.

The other side of this question is "what if I *always* want to have sex," which is the way many survivors feel at some point in their process. There are at least a couple of reasons why you might feel this way. No one really has a right to tell you what is "too much" sex for you. If the sex leaves you feeling genuinely good about yourself and your connection with your partner, then it is probably okay. But if *you* feel it is a problem, that is different.

Sometimes we want sex a lot because what we really want is to be close and to feel loved, and sex was the way we learned to get that kind of affection in childhood. Men sometimes have sex a lot because it gives them the sense that everything is okay. Being sexual is associated with being a healthy male, powerful and in control, producing at least the illusion of security.

Sometimes we want sex a lot because we do not think we are worth anything more than that. We may have learned that we could use sex as a reward to get something from someone else.

Again, there are ways to get needs met other than by sex. Nonsexual cuddling helps. Hugs help, too. Finding other things you do well and getting recognition for them works best of all. The questions to ask yourself are "What do I *really* want?" and "Is sex the way I want to get it?"

Therapists can make suggestions on how to deal with your sex life, but if they start offering to demonstrate, or suggest sex with them as a practice run or as a "surrogate," say no. If this happens, report the therapist to his or her licensing board. It is another form of sexual abuse and a betrayal of trust. Remember, we have the power to act in this situation.

What Should I Do When I'm in Different Kinds of Groups and They Say Totally Opposite Things?

That may sound like a strange question, but it happens. Most drug and alcohol abuse programs do not want their clients in separate individual therapy or in an independent group on another issue. They think there will be conflicts or that the therapy will provide the client with an emotional escape in a way that undermines their program. Based on their experience, they are also concerned that therapy on childhood sexual abuse may bring up feelings strong enough to threaten their clients' sobriety, or even their clients' lives.

Often survivor groups and therapists require that you be drug-free and sober for a least a year before beginning to work on childhood abuse issues. They want you to have experience in dealing with everyday problems while you are sober before tackling the past. It may seem like a contradiction: the alcohol and drug problem may be a way to escape from the pain of the past abuse, but most programs want you sober before dealing with the cause.

We have known survivors who have attended Alcoholics Anonymous meetings while participating in a survivor support group. It seemed helpful to them at the time. But individual circumstances vary.

The choice, ultimately, is up to you. Be aware that childhood memories and feelings can be so strong that you become self-destructive. If you have signed a contract or made a commitment to go by the rules of the program you are in, it is important to honor that commitment, both for your own sense of integrity and in recognition of the fact that there are good reasons for those rules. If there is a conflict and it is upsetting you or holding you back, decide which group seems to be helping the most and stay with that one for a period of time. The other issue can be the main focus next time.

Should I Confront the Abuser?

Before answering the question about confronting the abuser in your past, there are two other questions that you should answer for yourself: "What do I want from the abuser?" and "Whose agenda is being played out: mine, the group's, the therapist's, the abuser's, or some significant other's?"

Some groups and therapists encourage survivors to confront the abuser if he or she is reachable. They believe confrontation is a strong action the survivor can take that breaks the silence and helps the survivor to feel more in control.

But it doesn't always work out that way. Sometimes the result is more damage to the survivor. Unless you are very clear that you want only to reveal the secret or express your anger and that you do not care what the response is, the confrontation may only expose you to more manipulation by the abuser.

And some abusers are out of reach—dead or moved away to an unknown address.

Confronting the abuser can be done in less risky ways—by writing letters that are not mailed, or using role playing.

But if *you* choose to confront the person who abused you, try to structure the confrontation in a way that keeps you safe. Take other trusted people with you who understand the issues. If there is a family member who is an ally, meet with her or him first and ask for help in communicating with the rest of the family and/or the abuser.

Meet the abuser in neutral or protected territory, never on or near the abuser's territory. Be clear about your message. Be prepared for the abuser to deny that he or she ever did anything sexual or harmful to you. Be warned that the abuser may try to charm your support people and undermine your credibility. Recognize what you might want from the abuser, while knowing that you probably won't get it (he or she didn't give you what you wanted then, why start now?): Is an apology enough? Is money (perhaps to pay for your counseling) enough? A promise that he or she will seek counseling for the problem? Will you believe any promises he or she makes?

Not only does the abuser usually deny that he or she did anything wrong, often the rest of the family denies that anything happened. They may be angry at you for making them look at something painful and ugly, or for whatever guilt they may feel, whether they admit those feelings to you or not. Or they may just turn away, suggesting that the abuse doesn't matter because it happened so long ago and insisting that you not talk about it with them.

When the abuser is a brother or sister, the parents often cannot face the fact that one child is an abuser and another the victim. They may accuse you of trying to make them choose between their children.

As a result of any of these family reactions, you may be abandoned or feel abandoned by your family during and after any confrontation with the abuser. You have a right to be angry at the family members who didn't help and protect you when you were a child, and who denied or covered up the abuse. You have reason to be angry at the family members who continue to deny and won't support you now.

Many survivors feel that if we could only explain it clearly enough, say it well enough, our families will understand and love us again. But the reality is that no matter how well we say it, they may never understand or admit what happened and why it's so important to deal with now. The problem is not just ours, it was and is the family's, and it is the responsibility of everyone involved to deal with it.

A Letter from a Male Survivor to His Father, the Abuser

A letter may be an effective way to confront the abuser. This is an example of a letter a male survivor wrote to his abusing father and read aloud to his therapy group before mailing it. Writing this letter made the survivor feel able to express the rage he felt toward his father who had abused him sexually and taken away his childhood. Writing it made him feel powerful, but also safe. This survivor wanted to hurt his father like he was hurt and make him feel the shame he felt. It was part of his process of unburdening and relieving some of the responsibility the survivor felt for what happened.

Well Dad, you old son-of-a-bitch,

We finally get to sit down and talk. I am tired of feeling shitty all the time. I am tired of what people might think of me. I am tired of not having other male friends because I am afraid to be alone with another man. It has been hard for me to trust my own feelings, and to trust others with my feelings. I am good at art and other things that you always made fun of me doing. It has taken me a while but lately I am not afraid to try new things. I also have gone back to school, "YAH" your worst fear but I am not "better" than you or anyone else in the family, I just can get a better job.

I am going to a counseling service to find myself. The self you screwed up. The self you belittled. The self you dirtied. I want to be clean and make myself happy again. I am not proud of the things you have done to me, and I am not going to hide from them anymore, nor am I going to cover for you anymore, nor am I going to hide the pain inside anymore.

I am tired of living in a family where no one can have their own opinion, where what you say goes no matter what. I am just tired of you playing God all the time, and not caring what anyone else has to say, feel, think, or want to do. None of us were put on this earth for you to kick around any time you just felt like it. And I think the worst part about it is that sometimes I act just like you. And I hate myself because of it. I am tired of living with a family where everyone is trying to hide secrets that shouldn't have happened and shouldn't have been covered up in the first place.

Maybe that is why I feel guilty, or responsible for what happened to me, because I was afraid of you, and didn't tell anyone else the shitty, disgusting crap you did to me. As a human being I think you are one of the lowest people on earth. Anyone who could do that to another person let alone his own son. And then to show what a real asshole you are, you go and tell people that I am lying, that I am making up stories, that I need professional help. While I am getting professional help because of the shitty things you dared to do to me, I am sick of having to remember all the crap you have done to me, and having to relive all the crap you have done to me, and put me through. And I am getting pissed off at you for the hell that I have put my family through. And you have the nerve to tell me that none of the touching ever happened and that I am the one who is fucked up.

DON'T YOU DARE.

I have worked hard to get this far.

I know I can't ask you to respect me because you don't respect yourself. You really don't give a damn about me because you don't give a damn about yourself. Don't ever ask me to care about your feelings, because you don't care about mine. You don't care about my feelings now, just like you didn't care about my feelings when you were abusing me. I am learning to deal and live with the shit you have done to me, I don't think you will ever learn.

All I want to say is get away from me until you get help. I would like to wake up one morning and find out that this nightmare is over and that I never have to look at this problem again. I know that it won't be that way, cause I will always remember the sexual abuse, and that from time to time I will still have the nightmares, and that I will always have the scares, and that I will always feel a certain shittiness inside, and none of it will ever go away.

Unfortunately,

Your Son

Letters from a Sibling Incest Survivor

These letters were written by a woman survivor who was molested for 12 years by her brother. He was two years older than she. She now feels it is important to recognize that what makes abuse between siblings possible is a difference in power, not only age. The first letter was written in the first year of her process, the second two years later. Both were mailed. The brother never responded in any way. The mother maintained a two-year silence, after which the survivor initiated limited contact.

The letters were an important step for the survivor in realizing that she could separate from her family and choose not to obey their wishes in keeping the secret. The first letter helped her see that she could express her anger at the person who deserved it instead of letting it victimize her.

Brother:

Mom said that you have no idea why I refuse to see you or be around you. She said that she thought maybe I just focused all my anger at men on you. If anything, it's the reverse—what you did to me fills me with anger at most men, at any men who treat women the way you treated me. You know damn well that I'm talking about INCEST. You power-tripped me, beat me up, threatened me, used me for your garbage can, and tried to throw me away. You coerced me into sex with you over a period of years. When I came out to you as a lesbian, your only response was to try to claim responsibility for that, and I denied it. I still deny it. But the way you used me has indeed affected my life, mostly in ways I don't like.

And you're not going to just get off. A lot of my friends hate you. They've watched me get violently sick to my stomach talking about how you raped me again and again all the time messing with my head about caring about me. Telling me I was special while you forced me to give blow jobs to your friends, always with the threat that you'd tell and it would be my fault. If I thought I could win, I'd take you to court, but I think it was too long ago. But I want your wife to know, and Mom. I don't want to hurt them, but buster, you shit on me for a lot of years and you never said NOTHING! I just want them to know that you're a first class pathological jerk. I want your wife to keep an eye on your son—I wouldn't put it past you to molest him like you did me, except that maybe you're homophobic enough to leave him alone. If you had had a daughter, I would have spoken up a long time ago. If I had my way, you'd be sterilized, if not castrated. You don't deserve to have any kids.

I've been remembering a lot lately after having repressed memory for a long time. I remember you twisting my arm up behind my back and marching me off to the fields behind the railroad track where you shoved me down on a red ants' nest to fuck. I remember how I never felt good enough in the rest of the world's eyes, and how I grew up terrified that someone would find out if I let them get close to me as a friend, so not letting people get close, always having a wall between. I remember trying to rationalize my victimization, thinking that somewhere you loved me (isn't sex what people do who love each other?) when all you wanted was a place to stick your prick, and someone to feel more powerful than.

So why am I writing this? Just so there's no doubt in your mind about why I want nothing to do with you. I don't care whether you respond or not. I don't believe anything you have to say. I would love to wreck your life and flush it down the toilet. You better steer clear of me, golden boy, first-born son, asswipe. You owe me.

Your Sister

Dear Mom,

I wish I could say "Thanks" for your letter, but it's clear that you don't really want to hear about the brother-sister incest in our family. You seem to feel guilty, but I don't hate you.

As for your comment hoping I can find some love in my heart for you, that's just the hell of it. It would be much easier if I couldn't. It would be easier on me, in some ways, if I could just hate my brother for what he did to me, and you for refusing to listen or care or help or support me, then and now. But since I can't hate you and him—it's too destructive to me—the way I stay sane is to stay away. The thing that would change my attitude is for you to ask, to really want to know what happened and how you can help. I can recommend books and articles to read. I would hope that you would use your considerable influence on your son to get him into therapy before he gets caught molesting some other little kid—or his own, for that matter.

I don't keep on about this in order to make you feel like a bad mother or to make you feel guilty. I've told you lots of times that I often feel pretty good about who I am, and that I've seen you as a good role model, a strong, competent woman who can take care of herself—and did, with three kids for a number of years.

What would change my attitude, my need to stay away, would be for you to reach out, talk to me without blame. I can imagine this situation might be difficult for you (on the other hand, I imagine you shrugging your shoulders and thinking that it doesn't have anything to do with you), but I don't know. I interpret your silence as not caring. I have felt often in the last three years that nearly every time I reached out to you, I got my fingers stepped on. I tried very hard, for as long as I could, to respect your wish not to know what my brother did to me. But not talking about it meant feeling crazy, sometimes suicidal (I tried to overdose on painkillers the weekend of my sister's wedding, but didn't have enough of them to do more than make myself sick), and always isolated. For awhile it was really nice to connect with Uncle Bob—he's the only one of the family whose response was, "Gee, I'm really sorry that happened, it must have been very hard for you."

I can almost hear you thinking that I've been an adult for 11 years now, and I should be able to put the past behind me, that I'm being self-centered (your voice in my head adds, "as usual"). It's just not that simple. I know that everyone has a burden; some harder, some easier. You didn't exactly have an easy childhood either. But what would help me get this behind me is to be able to talk with you about it. Please write.

Your Daughter

Some families do listen and respond when a survivor tells them now what happened in the past. They may apologize, go into family therapy, and really try to help. However, it might not be enough and you may still be angry. Some families respond, and we can't really accept the response because we have learned not to trust.

A brief word here about lawsuits. Some survivors have tried to sue the family

members who abuse them. Other survivors have felt that continuing to try for reconciliation was more important to them than seeking court-ordered restitution. The results have been mixed. A young women sued her father in California as soon as she turned 18. Her suit was successful in that she received money and property. Another woman in her thirties sued her father in New York and lost her case when the judge ruled that too much time had gone by since the abuse. She has appealed.

Think it through. The dollar cost of suing is very high, though sometimes a lawyer will take a case based on a percentage of the damages he or she hopes the court will award, or because it might set an important precedent. There are lawyers' fees, fees for filing papers with the courts, travel expenses, payments for "expert" witnesses—such as therapists—fees for transcripts if you want to appeal an unsuccessful outcome.

The money *can* be found—from friends, support committees, and fundraising events if suing is important enough to you. And there is always the possibility that the abuser will offer you money to drop the suit before the case comes to trial. Whether you sue depends a lot on what you want.

Along with the dollar cost of a lawsuit, the emotional cost has to be figured as well. The public act of suing can be a boost—it feels like standing up for yourself and getting back at the abuser—with the added chance that a judge or jury (whose word carries much more weight than yours in the family and the community) will say out loud that the abuser did it and owes you something.

The defense lawyer will try to make it look like you asked for it, or you imagined it, or you are just plain lying. The abuser's lawyer may use any history you have of therapy or psychiatric hospitalization to discredit your testimony: "Don't believe her," he or she will imply to the jury, "she's obviously crazy."

Often a case is dismissed not because the facts are wrong, but because some technical rule was not followed. How will you deal with it if your case is thrown out of court? And are you prepared to have your name and picture in the newspaper next to the words "alleged victim of child sexual abuse"?

Weigh the costs carefully before you decide to sue. Try to find out as much as you can about your chances of success. If you go ahead, set up a strong support group for yourself: people who understand that every time your name is in the newspapers, it is like telling the secret all over again; people who will support you and tell you the truth no matter what; people who will protect you and run interference for you when you ask them to.

Should I "Forgive" the Abuser?

The real question here is who the forgiveness is for. Your job as a survivor is to teach the child inside how to be powerful and take care of yourself in the world, how to make real choices, how to ask for what you want, how to have feelings and satisfying relationships with good people. It is not your job any longer to take care of the abuser's feelings.

If you see "forgiving" the abuser as part of *your* process, a way of getting his or her negative influence out of your life after having fully explored your feelings, then yes, do it. That kind of forgiveness is something you can do within yourself, whether or not the abuser is accessible. You may decide to change how you relate to the abuser after coming to that forgiveness. Or you may not. You may try out what "forgiveness" feels like to you and discover that it does not make your anger disappear.

But if you are forgiving the abuser because the abuser asks you to, because your family, your therapist, your minister, priest or rabbi, or anyone else thinks you *should*, or because it's "part of the program," forget it. It probably would not be real, and it will only make you feel more guilty for still being angry and upset.

5
For Lovers and Others

Adults who were sexually abused as children have a pretty rough stretch of road ahead in their emotional lives as they begin to recall, relive, and reprocess that abuse. But the abuse affects lovers, close friends, and family members, too.

In this chapter, we will cover some of the questions lovers and others (marriage partners, sisters and brothers, close friends) ask, including how you can help survivors get over this rough road with the least damage to your relationships and how you—the survivor's close support people—can take care of yourselves, too.

The Abuse Was All in the Past, Why Is It Coming Up Now?

The past does not die as long as memory survives. Any small thing, a noise, a smell, a way of touching or being touched, can trigger memories of abuse. It might not have anything to do with you as a lover or family member, except that it affects your relationship. You may feel like you are walking on eggshells all the time, afraid that anything you do will trigger a flashback—an intense period of reliving the abuse, or some part of it, as if it were happening right now.

Flashbacks are probably the most frightening part of reprocessing abuse, though not everyone has them. They often make the survivor feel "crazy," and you may think he or she should be in a mental hospital because the experience is so intense and frightening.

Some survivors have "flashbacks" that you'd never know about unless they told you. It can be as simple as feeling frightened by a particular smell, and not understanding why, or avoiding certain places or foods because of the unexplained feelings they bring up. Perhaps the feelings are coming up now because you and the survivor have or know a child who is the age the survivor was when the abuse occurred.

Flashbacks, though painful, are not necessarily bad. They and other less intense memories of the abuse are occurring because in some way it is now safe for them to emerge. The memories had been hidden in order to help the abused child survive a horrible situation. They bring up feelings that need to be dealt with so the survivor can grow and change. Sometimes the best way to help the survivor is just to be there as though you were the safe, strong parent that your abused partner never had as a child.

That may also be the most difficult thing for you as a friend or partner. To watch someone you love go through such grief and pain, and yet know that you can't fix it, is one of the hardest things in the world to do. The survivor's grief and pain may frighten you, or remind you of some grief of your own. Sometimes, the lover or partner of a survivor begins to realize that he or she was molested as a child, too. Then it becomes doubly important for both of you to get outside help.

What Makes This So Different from Other Kinds of Painful Childhood Experiences?

Therapists are now beginning to realize that surviving sexual abuse is like surviving war—they call it "post traumatic stress syndrome." This war was started by an adult or older kid against a child whose sense of "self" was repeatedly invaded until the child could not understand anything about boundaries, could not establish or defend them. Often that violation was called "love." Even more confusing, it may have been accompanied by truly loving behavior in other areas of life.

You may have heard or read about how living with alcoholic parents affects children throughout their lives. The effects of sexual abuse are similar.

If you, as the lover or close friend of a survivor, can imagine how you would feel if you had been tricked and lied to in a way that affected your deepest sense of yourself—that made you believe you were guilty and worthless—for years by someone you had trusted, then you can begin to imagine part of what a survivor feels. The survivor has tried to build a self and a tolerable life on the foundation of emotional quicksand dumped there by the abuser. No wonder the structure feels unstable.

Your survivor friend or lover may appear incredibly strong, stable, helpful to others in crisis. There is a level on which that is all true. Despite the apparent—and real—strength, many survivors *feel* as if they are "faking it," that it's an "act," a performance they had to learn in order to hold their lives together. Sometimes helping others was the only way they could feel good about themselves in the face of the abuse, the only way they knew that others would like them. But when a survivor's entire sense of self worth is built on the opinions of others, she or he may look good, while feeling totally insecure.

That does not mean that your needs, your concerns about your own life always have to give way to the survivor's pain. You deserve care and attention, too. But you might not be able to get them from the survivor for a while. Just as the survivor has to recognize her or his own boundaries and begin to say "no," you have the right to say, "I'm sorry, I just can't deal with this right now. It doesn't mean I don't love you, it just means I can't help you with this."

This can be an opportunity to begin to look at yourself and discover what you need. You may find a new balance in your relationship after this time of struggle. The important thing is to get through the struggle. Have patience. Give yourselves as much time as you need.

How Can I Help?

Perhaps the first question to ask is "*Can* I help?". The answer is "Maybe, sometimes." You cannot make it up to the survivor and you cannot create a world in which she or he was never abused. That may be what many survivors secretly wish for in their heart of hearts. But that is not your job. Most of the ways in which you *can* help have more to do with taking some of the outside pressures off so that the survivor can safely go through the process, and finding ways to communicate love, respect and understanding even through pain and struggle.

You can help by believing the survivor when she or he tells you about having been abused. You can help by not treating the survivor like a freak, or like "damaged goods," or like someone with a disease. Accept that you cannot fix it. No one can fix it. But you and the survivor can learn to come to terms with it and to decrease its impact on your lives. Communication is the key.

Reading this chapter, the rest of this book, and/or other books about childhood sexual abuse can help by taking a big burden off the survivor in having to explain everything that's going on. It also tells the survivor that she or he is not alone in dealing with this problem and that you care enough to spend time and effort to try to understand. Just remember there are many theories, but only one expert on your partner's experience; she or he alone really knows what happened and how it feels.

What makes helping difficult is that your needs are not very important to the survivor right now. She or he is absorbed in memories and feelings and may have little energy or attention to give to you. You may feel discounted, rejected, or invisible, just when you may also feel frightened about the intensity of the feelings the survivor is experiencing—or you may be worried about your relationship as well as going through your own feelings.

What Do I Do with *My* Feelings?

Sometimes it's easier to be angry on someone else's behalf than to feel angry for yourself. Once you have heard and believed the survivor's history, you may feel all the rage with which the survivor is barely in touch. You may feel overwhelmed by that rage, or obsessed with imagining or knowing all the details of the abuse.

When the survivor is part of a family that includes the abuser, it is *not* your job to confront or expose the abuser in the community or in the family, no matter how angry you are. The only exception is if you have evidence that the abuser is currently molesting children. Then it is not your special job as the lover or friend of a survivor, but the job of any responsible adult to report it to the appropriate social service agency, not out of revenge or rage, but out of concern. It is, after all, your friend or lover's pain, childhood trauma, and sense of shame you would be exposing, as well as the abuser.

Just as it's not your job to "fix" the abuse, it is not the survivor's job to "fix" your feelings. The survivor has plenty of new and terrifying feelings to deal with. And sometimes the survivor may interpret your anger as directed at her or him as the "cause" of all the turmoil.

At times your survivor/partner may accuse you of acting like the abuser, or you may lash out when you feel rejected or unjustly accused. Nobody ever said that being with a survivor would be easy. But just as it is not the survivor's job to meet everyone else's needs all the time, neither is it always your job to be the parent, to be "big."

You may also feel that it's not fair—the survivor may be getting a lot of help and attention from therapists and close friends, while you aren't getting any support for your part: taking up the slack in your daily lives, feeling abandoned by your survivor/partner, and all the small and large ways you absorb the disruptions in your relationship. You may feel your own sense of rage at the abuser who hurt the one you love, as well as a sense of powerlessness that you can't change this thing that so affects your life and your relationship. But these are feelings that the survivor shouldn't have to deal with. You need to get nonjudgmental support for your feelings, too.

Your concerns and frustrations are real. Living with a survivor of child sexual abuse is often difficult. There is a fine line between giving a survivor respect, understanding and sympathy, and treating the survivor as though the only way she or he can get attention is by continuing to be a victim. Being overprotective can be as bad as ignoring the effects of the abuse. Sometimes talking with others who live with survivors helps to put the situation in perspective.

Like support groups for survivors, a support group for lovers and spouses of survivors provides a source of information and relief from feeling alone. It helps tremendously to hear other people say, "We went through that, and here is how we worked it out," or even, "We are going through that too, and I don't know what to do."

But perhaps the most important message a support group can give to lovers and spouses of survivors is that you cannot fix the abuse. It's not your fault that you cannot fix the abuse. You are not causing this pain or these memories, even if something you did may have triggered them. It is something the survivor has to work out.

There are few groups so far for partners of survivors. But the need is there and they are being established. If there isn't one in your town, start one. You don't necessarily need a therapist, but you do need to make sure that meetings do not degenerate into general "trash the victim" sessions. The object is understanding the survivor and yourself, and helping you get your needs met.

What Kinds of Changes Might Occur in Our Relationship During This Process?

Change is difficult, but necessary. The survivor may have tried very hard to please you, and now that is changing. It feels uncomfortable. You probably fight more. But every time your partner says no or asserts the new self, it is a healthy sign. If you want a co-operative relationship, have patience. If you want a relationship where your needs count the most, then it is probably going to be very difficult for you to support the survivor through these changes.

There may be wild swings in your relationship. A male survivor who has just begun to talk about having been abused may be wide open emotionally for the first time. Then, in part because men are taught to turn off emotions, he may be even more distant than before.

These changes may happen several times, but each time it will get easier to recognize what is going on. What helps is for each of you to talk to the other as openly as possible.

A female survivor who has always been a caretaker may not want to take care of anyone but herself during this process. Or she, who was always so open emotionally, may become distant and closed. You, her female or male partner, can talk about respecting the need for the change, and how it affects you. When you say you feel rejected, the survivor may be surprised—it is not what she intended. You can then accept that she is not rejecting *you*, just taking some space.

A male survivor who is shut down and distant can tell you he wants some space to work things out and not just disappear. You, his female or male partner, can tell him that his feelings are not bad, and you really want to know what he's feeling, really want to understand. You can tell him how it affects you when he disappears emotionally. Communication is much easier when it happens in the context of trust.

"Trust" covers a lot of things. You are a trusted person in the survivor's life. You may not *feel* trusted, but since the survivor—with good reason—rarely trusts anyone deeply, you may have to accept that the survivor trusts you as much as possible at that point.

Maintaining trust includes always being honest, keeping promises, respecting limits, and accepting differences. Many things get in the way of being able to do this in a relationship when so much turmoil is going on. Just remember that this is a process, that things will change, and that you have the right to say no. If you can communicate your feelings and listen to each other while also allowing the process to continue, you will have a better chance for your relationship to improve and change as each of you change.

How Long Does It Take for Survivors to Get Better—When Will My Partner Be "Normal" Again?

That's a question for which there is not just one answer. How long depends in part on how long the abuse lasted, in part on how violent the abuse was, in part on how young the survivor was then, whether or not the child told someone and was believed, and how the parents dealt with the abuse. It depends on how many strengths the survivor has to build on now, and on whether or not friends, family, and lover can give constructive support.

Let us look at what "returning to normal" means. First, what does "normal" mean? If it means "like everyone else," your partner or friend is already a lot like other people. While real numbers may be much higher, studies give a conservative estimate that more than one out of nine women in this country have been sexually assaulted in childhood by a relative and that even more have been subjected to indecent exposure, fondled, molested, or raped as children by someone outside the family. Men are also sexually abused in childhood, more frequently than current data indicate. Therefore, the way your partner is and what she/he is going through is absolutely "normal" for a significant percentage of the population—those who have been sexually abused.

But if "normal" means "the way she/he was before she/he started talking about the abuse," the answer to "returning to normal" is probably never. The process is about building a *new* identity, replacing an old one built on lies, secrets, and shame. You cannot go back to innocence. Those memories are there, influencing the actions of the survivor, whether they get talked about or not.

The other important word in that question about being "normal" is "again." When a child is abused there is no real base on which to build right-and-wrong, yes-and-no. Because of the abuse, there never was a "normal" for the survivor. Life was built on lies. What is happening now is building a sense of "normal" that is entirely new.

But this process does not have to take over your entire lives. Many days or weeks or months can feel normal. It is a lot like grief, overwhelming at first, but as the reservoir of hidden, dammed-up feelings begins to flow more fully, the pressure and the volume of grief gradually decrease. In a very real way, the survivor is grieving for an innocent childhood that her or his abuser killed with the abuse.

It's normal for people in this society to expect that hard problems will have instant solutions. But in real life it takes longer than one hour with commercial interruptions. Give your partner enough time. Give yourself enough time. Have patience. It's worth it.

There is no set answer to "how long?" but there is hope. The survivor may take as long to heal as the abuse did to occur. One survivor we know was abused for 12 years. She's been talking about it with friends and in therapy for about six years and feels more fully real in the world, with happiness and satisfaction in the choices she makes. The process may not be "over," but it is rare for the memories of the abuse to overwhelm and paralyze her as they did in the beginning. She has been in a stable relationship for eight years; she and her life partner recently bought a house together.

Not every relationship is entered into with the idea that it will continue indefinitely. Some relationships are just for fun, others are learning experiences and others were intended to be short term. Being with a survivor in a short-term relationship can be exhilarating, fulfilling, and wonderful, along with all the emotional work. Remember it is not your job to rescue the survivor, or to stay in the relationship until the survivor is "done" with the work.

If you are in a long-term relationship with a survivor, you are likely to see more of the process and more of the changes. The person who emerges will probably be somewhat different from the person you knew at the beginning. And you may also be changed by your part in the process. Life is change, and it can be exciting.

What About Relationships with Families of Origin?

Again, it depends on the circumstances. When the abuser is alive and part of the survivor's family, the survivor may not want to have any contact with that family. That wish should be respected.

The survivor may at some point want to confront the abuser, either by letter or in person. That may be healing for the survivor, a way of taking back her or his own life from the domination of the abuser. Your support can make all the difference in the world as to how painful the process is. Remember that the survivor needs to make the choice, when and if she or he is ready, no matter how much you think they should do it "for their own good."

One way you can help is by asking the survivor questions about what she or he wants from the confrontation, or whether she or he will believe anything the abuser and other family members say. The survivor may be welcome in the family only if she or he does not talk about the abuse. The abuser, when confronted, often denies that any sexual activity took place, calls it innocent "cuddling," suggests that you mind your own business—it is a family matter, or tells you in a confiding tone that since childhood your lover has always made up stories like this to get sympathy and attention.

Abusers are often charming and extremely skillful at manipulating others. You must not be taken in. Remember that your alliance is with the survivor, and nothing the abuser says should shake that support.

Remember how powerful the sexually abusive family system can be. The denial may be so strong that even when the survivor's memories of what happened are crystal clear, contact with the family brings in doubt that the abuse really occurred and thoughts that maybe she or he really did make it up or just dreamed it. The survivor has lived with this all of her or his life—frequent reality checks from you that you know and believe it really happened, and that the survivor is not crazy, will help.

An Abuser's Silent Partner Speaks*

The following is an actual letter written to a member of Survivors of Incest Anonymous, by her mother. Her mother knew of the incest and did not adequately protect her four daughters from their father's sexual advances. Very little has been changed except for clarity's sake.

Since the time that this letter was written, both mother and daughter have started therapy together. This is truly a courageous act and we commend both of them. Hopefully, another letter may be sent, a more appropriate letter where flattery isn't mixed with insults and where self-sacrifice isn't confused with loyalty; where limits are placed on human relationships; and rape and its painful consequences is NOT considered an acceptable and insignificant part of family life; a letter where her mother takes responsibility for herself and her own recovery. Then her mother will be on the road to becoming a survivor also.

My Dearest Daughter,

I have this feeling within that now is the time for me, as your mother, to tell you the love and gratitude in my heart for you as one of my children but especially for you, who have always stood beside me thru thick and thin. You have stood by me at times when I should never have asked, any other child

* © 1985 Survivors of Incest Anonymous (SIA). Reprinted with permission.

would have told me exactly what I could do with my pleas. You have lied when I needed that, paid bills that everyone helped make, made me feel beautiful when I looked like "shit." You have suffered indignity, humiliation at the hands of an animal you call Dad, that I allowed to happen. I will ask you to forgive me and tell you that I have been weak, I guess I have used the strength of you, my child. I love you very much though I have had a poor way of showing my love. I will always remember your love for me and always be there when you need me, if you want me to be. I guess I will always remember the roses and the note you and your sisters sent me, "To the best friend four sisters ever had." Any mother would and could be proud to have you for their daughter, but I win again, you are mine and only death will cause us to part. Still a part of you would probably watch over me when I'm gone to make sure I'd stay out of trouble, for that's your nature. Caring, loving, forgiving, anything goes when it comes to your mom.

I am one lucky mother to have you for my daughter. I love you now and I will love you forever.

Mom
Mother

The survivor may also have a hard time relating to *your* family of origin. The feelings may range from coldness or rejection of your family, to an obsessive desire to please or impress them. You can help by providing a realistic picture of your family and reminding the survivor that it is not her or his job to impress your family and that they have not volunteered to become her or his family too. It is another lesson in helping the survivor understand boundaries and separate identities.

Partners, friends, lovers, and families of survivors may have more questions or feelings about what the survivor is going through. You deserve answers. There are books in libraries or in some bookstores that can help you understand more of what happened to the survivor and what she or he might be feeling about it. Check the reading list in Appendix A for suggestions.

You may also want to talk once or several times to a therapist or counselor who has experience with clients who are survivors. If the survivor in your family is seeing a therapist or counselor, you need to ask permission before seeing the same counselor the survivor is seeing. Seeing the same counselor might feel like trespassing on the survivor's safe space, violating her or his boundaries. Or it may feel like a relief to have the counselor explain things that the survivor cannot. Just the fact that you want to know and understand may feel like help to the survivor.

6
Surviving Systems

"Systems" are really groups of laws, rules or organizations for dealing with a problem. The people who carry out or abide by those laws and rules also become part of the system. Some of them do very good work, not just in carrying out the rules, but in trying to make the system work for people.

The three systems that survivors of child sexual abuse often come into contact with are the mental health system, the social services system, and the legal or "justice" system. In most cases, these are state or county systems. However, mental health and social services may also be offered by private agencies that receive funds from foundations or public giving. Most of the people who are likely to come into contact with public services are those without money or other resources either temporarily or on a long-term basis. While that doesn't mean the quality of what they offer is lower than in private services, it sometimes adds a level of power and threat. Although these systems are ideally meant to help people, sometimes they end up controlling people instead. That makes everyone, not only former victims of abuse, feel powerless and frustrated.

Agencies and systems, like the individual people in them, sometimes base their actions on what is called a "hidden agenda," an unwritten set of assumptions, goals and rules that may interfere with your getting the help you want. Hidden agendas change constantly with different circumstances. For the purposes of illustration, let's say you have an appointment at 4:00, and the office closes at 4:30. The acknowledged agenda, or purpose, for the appointment is to discuss what options are available to you and to make decisions about them. If you are unable to make those decisions before closing time, the worker may start to push you to make quicker decisions, or just to follow his or her recommendations. Instead of helping you to make the best decisions for you, the caseworker's "hidden agenda" becomes wanting to leave at quitting time.

But you can survive these systems; you may even get some help from them, though in some cases it may not be the kind of help you most want or need. The best way to use a system to get what you need is to know what it is set up to do (what its written and unwritten agendas are), whether anything on those agendas will help you (what you want), and how to get out of the system.

For survivors involved in these systems, it may be hard to understand that no single agency or worker can make everything all right, not even the best and most caring of them. Usually the best they can do is tell you what is available and try to help you get it.

The second hardest thing for survivors to understand is that the system wasn't set up to make life difficult for us in particular. Since most systems are set up for the convenience of the providers, everyone—even the most competent, least traumatized person—has a hard time. Friends who have been through these systems, legal advocates, and others who know how the systems work, can help you by sharing their information.

Mental Health

State-operated mental health systems usually have a number of items on their agendas, one of which is to help you feel better. But because they are state funded and must offer a wide variety of services, the agencies may place other issues higher in priority.

Some of the agenda items (not necessarily in order of priority) for state mental health agencies are:

Collecting information and statistics. You walk into your local mental health agency and speak to an "intake worker," who may immediately ask you a lot of very personal questions about why you are there. If you refuse to answer, you may get labeled "withdrawn" or "uncooperative," or may not be allowed to see a counselor.

You have the right to ask for and write down the name of the intake worker. You can ask the reason for questions which seem too personal or offensive and decide whether it is for a good enough reason to answer. You can ask what happens if you refuse to answer any or all of the questions, and decide if that is worse than answering. Ask where the information is kept, who sees it, and what happens to the file after you are not a client any more. Ask the counselor whether you can see your own file and any notes the counselor takes while seeing you. Ask what kind of supervision the counselor has, who it is with, and how your counselor discusses cases with that supervisor.

Ask these questions of any counselor you see, not just public mental health workers.

Many public and private agencies now have to tell you what your rights are when you come for services. These include your right to privacy, your right to know and agree or disagree with the treatment plan, how much the services will cost, how you can file complaints if necessary, and what kinds of information cannot by law be kept confidential.

Drug and alcohol treatment. Most states have budgeted money to treat people who depend on illegal drugs and alcohol. Often the treatment is required after someone is arrested for drunk or drugged driving, for exhibitionism, or for some minor crime. If money for drug and alcohol treatment makes up most of an agency's budget, then people with those problems and people referred by the police or the courts will get the most attention and energy.

You may need or want to use one of these services if you are having some problems with alcohol or drugs. If so, this may still not be the place to start. Often chemical dependency treatment centers are not interested in whether you are a victim of sexual abuse. They focus on the chemical use and regard other issues as excuses or diversions. But usually the chemical abuse has become a means of coping with the pain of what happened. You may find yourself trapped in the middle: because of the overwhelming feelings involved, abuse treatment programs and groups usually work only with clients who have been sober and drug-free for six months to a year. Do the best you can. You may find a therapist who will help you with the abuse while you're in the drug or alcohol treatment program, though many therapists agree it is best to deal with one issue at a time. Later you may find a group where you can work on the abuse after you've made progress on the drug or alcohol problem.

Suicide prevention. At times, survivors may feel suicidal. Many public mental health agencies offer confidential suicide hotlines for adults and teenagers. It is another area of concern that often receives money from the state budget. When you reveal in face-to-face counseling that you are feeling suicidal and are likely to act on the feeling, the most extreme response may be to commit you to a state mental institution until you are not a "threat" to yourself or others.

There are laws governing who can be committed and for how long. Usually an involuntary commitment is for 72 hours. After that time, you get a hearing before a judge to determine whether you are a threat to yourself or to someone else. If not, they must let you go. To protect your rights you are usually entitled to have a lawyer represent you at this hearing.

But in practice, it may be difficult for a judge to tell the difference between your anger and pain at the abuse and being committed against your will, and whether or not you are a real threat to your own safety.

Sometimes, when the immediate crisis is over, you may get shuffled off to another agency or another counselor rather than getting to deal with the real underlying problem.

Control of "symptoms." The agency's written or unwritten agenda may include trying to get you "functional" by controlling your "symptoms." Mental health services that are funded by your employer may have a bias toward prescribing drugs that mask your symptoms and change your behavior so you can function in a job. There may be valid reasons to help you get or keep a job—having a job and a steady paycheck can help you feel better about yourself.

Some survivors have been helped at various times by taking therapeutic drugs. Because an agency—or any private therapist, for that matter—prescribes anti-depressants, tranquilizers or other drugs does not necessarily imply poor quality counseling. Again, it is your right to ask questions: What is the name of the drug? What is it supposed to do? What are its side-effects? What happens if I refuse to take it? Who pays for this prescription? How big is the dose? How will you know if the dose is right? How will you decide when I should stop taking it?

Groups and other resources. Because a state agency keeps records on clients and sees so many people, it can easily coordinate groups for clients, incest survivors' groups being a good example. When there is a good, well-trained, sensitive leader, group counseling can be very helpful. Ask at your intake visit whether the agency has or knows of any groups for survivors that are free or do not cost much. Ask what the requirements are to be in a group. Ask for a referral.

Most of all, ask questions. *You have a right to understand what is happening and what it means to you.*

Social Services

A state's social service system usually includes welfare and child protective services, as well as services for the physically handicapped and other groups in need of state resources. Social service agencies are staffed by professional social workers. They may be the best source of information about the programs available through your county or state, including residential treatment homes where you could live temporarily and receive help, crisis drop-in centers that are staffed 24 hours a day, or help with parenting problems.

Adult survivors may come into contact with any of several branches of social services, but here we will focus on child protective services. It is the program that *should* have helped us as children, and the system in which we are most likely to feel powerless, since our contact with them would most likely be in dealing with the abuse or neglect of our own children.

Child protective service agencies have as their sole concern the well-being of children up to age 18 or 21. As with all state services, that concern is limited and shaped by the laws and rules state social service workers must follow. Rules vary from state to state.

In some states, after investigation, a child protective service worker cannot force a family member accused of incest or other abuse out of the home. They usually can, however, remove a child who is being abused from the home into protective custody, placing the child in a juvenile group home or in short-term foster care. They may or may not be required to make a report or referral to other state services or agencies that will offer counseling to the abuser or restrain or restrict his or her access to the child.

The child, though, often feels like she or he is "bad" and being punished by being taken away from the family. Those feelings can be overcome when the foster care placement is short term and not repeated, when the foster family is well trained and highly compassionate, and when the state offers counseling services to the child victim.

Too often, however, that is not the case. Among adult survivors we have spoken with, stories have emerged of sexual abuse continuing in the foster home, especially when the foster family is informed of the reason for the child's placement. Some states do not have enough foster homes for the kids who need them. Some may have other safe places to send children at risk of abuse, while others may not.

Just remember that your idea of what the child needs and social service's idea may be very different. That does not mean your idea is bad or wrong and theirs is "right."

Legal or "Justice" System

Courts are actually about laws, and not necessarily about true "justice," making things right. Courts are not necessarily fair and there is a limit to what they can do. If you are seeking help through the courts, it is important that you keep reminding yourself of those facts.

Adult survivors who are not acting out their anger by committing crimes are most likely to come into contact with the courts in seeking relief-from-abuse orders, prosecuting an abuser who is charged with molesting your children, suing the original abuser of an adult survivor, and divorce and child custody.

Because the rules are so different in each state, we can't discuss each of these things individually. But there is one general rule: GET HELP. Just as there are doctors who, when they are doing their jobs well, act as sources for information and as advocates within the large, specialized and bewildering system of a hospital, there are lawyers and advocates whose job is to help you get through the court system.

But there are also lawyers who represent the state's interest, which may not be the same as yours. They are called "prosecutors," "district attorneys," or "state's attorneys." When you are the victim of a crime, whether it is child abuse or something else, these lawyers are not necessarily trying to set things right with you. They are trying to follow the laws of the state. Some state's attorneys are elected— that means that political issues may become part of the hidden agenda.

Although courts are set up by the government to administer justice, they can be insensitive to the emotional cost of testifying for adult or child victims of abuse. Being involved in the court process can bring up old feelings of being helpless and powerless. The courtroom itself may be an intimidating place to both adult and child. Therefore, it is important to find a competent public defender or private lawyer with whom you feel comfortable as well as an advocate or friend who can go with you to your lawyer's office and to court. Such a friend can visit the empty court-room with you so it won't feel so strange. She or he can help you make decisions, can help ask the right questions when you're confused by legal language, can remind you that even when it looks like there are no choices, you always have the choice of stopping or leaving.

In addition to private victim-advocate services that may be available, most states have some type of Victim Assistance Program (see Appendix B). Professionals trained in criminal court procedures or in civil court strategies can steer you through the gobbledygook of legal language and processes and spare you some of the trauma caused by exposure to the criminal justice system. Just remember *you don't have to go it alone—someone is there to help you.*

With a few exceptions, courts seem to operate the same way an abuser does: "I'm bigger and stronger than you, so you have to do what I say." The group that began the work for this book envisioned what we want real justice to do:

To protect everyone from being abused.

To state clearly and firmly that abuse will not be tolerated in our community.

To hold abusers responsible for their acts.

To place *no blame* on victims who are not committing crimes.

To retrain abusers so they never again consider children as sexual objects.

To provide a relapse-prevention program for abusers monitored by a responsible person or agency.

To provide restitution for the victim/survivor: money, because that represents the ability to get help; emotional restitution, beginning with an apology from the abuser; and open-ended counseling.

To provide a long-term ally for the victim/survivor within the legal system in case of further abuse.

To require training for police, prosecutors, lawyers, and judges on all issues involved in abuse, especially those of responsibility and power.

Some states have programs that include some of these ideas. Others have made progress in such areas as making it easier for child victim/witnesses to testify by allowing video-taped testimony, and extending the statute of limitations for sexual abuse crimes. They got those programs and those legal changes because people like us—like you—asked for them, demanded them, lobbied for them. They have those programs because we dared to dream of changing the world.

7
Changing the World

Many of the survivors involved in the creation of this book, and many more we met in groups and at conferences and workshops, are out to change the world, to help children who are now being abused, and to help prevent any more abusers from victimizing children. It is a tall order, but it is not impossible.

In fact, some survivors find that working to change the world makes them feel better, more powerful, even while they are processing their past.

Changing the world takes many forms. Writing letters to newspapers in response to articles on child abuse helps spread new information. Speaking out in public on your experience does the same. Two good places to speak are in college classes (usually listed as "Dynamics of the Family," or "The Dysfunctional Family," within the departments of Sociology or Psychology), and in workshops and conferences on child sexual abuse for professionals.

The "helping professionals"—therapists, social workers, doctors, and nurses—are used to seeing women as *victims*. Therefore, it can be very powerful and effective for women survivors who are strong and competent to present testimony. And because these professionals see men much less often as victims, it is important for male survivors to tell their personal histories to professional groups.

While there is more awareness now that males are also sexually abused, the personal story of a survivor is one of the most effective ways to educate others. One man who risked being interviewed on a local TV news program about his victimization said it helped in his own recovery. While at first he felt quite anxious following the broadcast, he received a lot of support from friends who had seen the program. Later, he reported feeling emotionally stronger and less ashamed.

The most difficult thing about speaking at conferences is the feeling that the researchers, therapists, and social workers speak a language that you may not understand. They use jargon to put labels on parts of an experience that you know from the inside. They may say things about child sexual abuse that do not fit your life, that feel untrue. They may tell jokes—because the issues they deal with constantly are so painful—or show attitudes that feel so uninvolved or offensively patronizing that you feel like you are under a microscope, or under attack.

Other therapists and researchers have respectfully recognized adult survivors as a major source of information on the long-term effects of abuse. Our histories help them see where the systems that were supposed to help failed. Our insights suggest areas where new ideas should be tried.

It is not easy, and sometimes it is very scary. But each time you confront future or practicing social workers and therapists, lawyers, pediatricians or whomever, with the live reality of sexual abuse and its effects on your adult life, you are making it harder for sexual abuse to be kept secret. You are making it easier for them to remember that the quality of their work and their caring will make a huge difference in some child's later life. And you are helping future child victims to get better help, sooner, with less pain.

Many states have laws making it so difficult for children to testify against abusers, that few abusers are ever taken to court. They may have no training programs for foster families on helping children who have been sexually abused. They may have no treatment programs for young sex offenders who, if not dealt with now, may harbor a strong potential to abuse others. They have "statute of limitation" laws that prevent adults who were victimized as children from suing the person who abused them because too much time has gone by.

These are all areas where, by writing letters to state lawmakers and testifying in hearings, you can help change the world, by changing the laws in your part of it.

But perhaps the most important way to change the world is much closer to home: being a safe friend to a needy child; being a supportive friend to a confused and scared adult who is living in an abusive situation; believing that what they tell you is true; and encouraging and helping them to take action. We may not be able to save the whole world or all those in it who need help. But we can make a difference for the next generation, while at the same time learning how strong, powerful and effective we can be. *We do not have to be powerless any more.*

Afterword

The careful process involved in the conceptualization and writing of *Adults Molested as Children: A Survivor's Manual for Women & Men,* the first self-help publication written by sexual abuse survivors for both female and male survivors, is integral to the spirit in which it was conceived.

The idea for the manual originated at a small conference organized by The Safer Society Program of the New York State Council of Churches in Shoreham, Vermont, in February 1986. Participants, all women, were equally divided between mental health professionals working with survivors of child sexual abuse and survivors themselves who had publicly written or spoken on the issues involved, or both. They included the following persons who, with one exception, continued to serve as an advisory committee through the completion of the publication:

Euan Bear, writer and founder and convenor of the first peer support group for incest survivors in Vermont,

Sallie O. Davis, counseling social worker at the Child Abuse Prevention Center in Pittsburgh, Pennsylvania, whose concerns on these issues precipitated the conference,

Anne-Marie Eriksson, Board Chair of Incest Survivors Resource Network, International, and former New York probation officer,

Ruth Friedman, counseling social worker at the Child Abuse Prevention Center in Pittsburgh, Pennsylvania,

Karen Dashiff Gilovich, therapist at Family and Children's Service of Ithaca, New York,

Jo Ann Yolanda Hernandez, author of "Long Range Consequences of Incest," and Vermont graduate student,

Fay Honey Knopp, the conference convenor, researcher, writer, and advocate, and director of The Safer Society Program,

Faith Lowell, psychotherapist in private practice in Middlebury, Vermont, and a community educator on issues of family and sexual violence, and

Asiba Tupahache, editor of the *Longhouse Newsletter of the Matinecock Nation* and author of *Taking Another Look* who enlarged our awareness of cultural issues involved in incest, but decided not to continue serving on our advisory committee.

Kim Altermatt Storm, a member of the Survivor's Caucus of the National Coalition Against Sexual Assault, was unable to attend the conference, but contributed through comments and a personal taped interview in Minnesota.

The conferees outlined the issues to be addressed in the self-help manual. The outline was used subsequently as a basis for several workshops and interviews with adult male survivors.

After Euan Bear completed writing the first draft of the manual, Peter Dimock, a St. Paul, Minnesota social worker and survivor who specializes in the treatment of adult male survivors, provided additional perspectives specific to males. The manuscript was then circulated to the advisory committee members and was read and commented on by the following readers: Lauren Berrizbeitia, Judy Breitmeyer, Don Cotton, Anne-Marie Eriksson, Erik A. Eriksson, Karen Dashiff Gilovich, Kevin Gregerson, Faith Lowell, Robin Mide, Jo Schneiderman, Ken Singer, Margaret Stinson, and Jim Struve. The final content of this manual is the responsibility of Euan Bear and Fay Honey Knopp and does not necessarily reflect the opinions of all of the readers.

Appendix A

Bibliography

About adults abused as children. (1987). South Deerfield, MA: Channing L. Bete.

Bass, E., & Davis, L. (1988). *The courage to heal: A guide for women survivors of child sexual abuse.* New York: Harper & Row.

Bass, E., & Thornton, L. (Eds.) (1983). *I never told anyone.* New York: Harper & Row.

Blume, E.S. (1990). *Secret survivors: Uncovering incest and its aftereffects in women.* New York: John Wiley and Sons.

Bronson, C. (1989). *Growing through the pain.* Park Ridge, IL: Parkside Publishing.

Butler, S. (1979). *Conspiracy of silence: The trauma of incest.* New York: Bantam Books.

Caruso, B. (1986). *Healing: A handbook for adult victims of sexual abuse.* Beverly Caruso, 2829 Inglewood Avenue South, Minneapolis, MN 55416.

Childhelp USA (1988). *Survivor's guide.* Los Angeles Child Help Center, P.O. Box 630, Hollywood, CA 90028.

Davis, L. (1990). *The courage to heal workbook: For women and men survivors of sexual abuse.* New York: Harper & Row.

Dimock, P.T. (1988). Adult males sexually abused as children: Characteristics and implications for treatment. *Journal of Interpersonal Violence, 3,* (2), 203-221.

Evert, K. & Bijkerk, I. (1987). *When you're ready.* Walnut Creek, CA: Launch Press.

Fairchild, R. (1987, Feb. 1). Personal communication.

Fisher, S.F. (1985). Identity of two: The phenomenology of shame in borderline development and treatment. *Psychotherapy, 22* (1),101-109.

Forward, S., & Buck, C. (1979). *Betrayal of innocence.* New York: Penguin Books.

Gil, E. (1983). *Outgrowing the pain: A book for and about adults abused as children.* Walnut Creek, CA: Launch Press.

Grubman-Black, S.D. (1990). *Broken boys/mending men: Recovery from childhood sexual abuse.* Tab Books, Blue Ridge Summit, PA 17294-0850 (1-800-822-8138).

Herman, J.L. (1981). *Father-daughter incest.* Cambridge, MA: Harvard University Press.

Hernandez, J.A.Y. (1985). *Long range consequences of incest.* Unpublished manuscript.

Hutchinson, M.A. (1985). *Characteristics: Survivors of incest.* Marilyn A. Hutchinson, Ph.D., 2161 McGee, Kansas City, MO 64113.

Justice, B., & Justice, R. (1979). *The broken taboo: Sex in the family.* New York: Human Sciences Press.

Lew, M. (1990). *Victims no longer: Men recovering from incest and other sexual child abuse.* New York: Harper & Row.

Maltz, W., & Holman, B. (1987). *Incest and sexuality: A guide to understanding and healing.* Lexington, MA: Lexington Books.

McNaron, T., & Morgan, Y. (1982). *Voices in the night: Women speaking about incest.* Minneapolis, MN: Cleis Press.

Miller, A. (1984). *For your own good.* New York: Farrar, Strauss, Giroux.

Morris, M. (1982). *If I should die before I wake.* New York: J.P. Tarcher.

Narimanian, R. (1990). *Secret feelings and thoughts: A book about male victimization by sexual abuse.* Philly Kids Play It Safe, 1421 Arch Street, Philadelphia, PA 19102-1582, (215) 686-8785.

Porter, E. (1986). *Treating the young male victim of sexual assault: Issues & intervention strategies.* Orwell, VT: Safer Society Press.

Randall, M. (1987). *This is about incest.* Ithaca, NY: Firebrand Books.

Roberts, L. (1987). *A treatment manual for therapy groups with survivors of childhood incest.* Rape Crisis Center, Inc., 147 South Butler Street, Madison, WI 53703.

Rush, F. (1980). *The best kept secret: Sexual abuse of children.* Englewood Cliffs, NJ: Prentice-Hall.

Russell, D.E.H. (1986). *The secret trauma: Incest in the lives of girls and women.* New York: Basic Books.

Sanford, L.T. (1980). *The silent children: A parent's guide to the prevention of child sexual abuse.* Garden City, NY: Anchor Press.

Sanford, L.T., & Donovan, M.E. (1984). *Women and self-esteem: Understanding and improving the way we think and feel about ourselves.* Garden City, NY: Anchor Press/Doubleday.

Satullo, J.A.W., Russell, R., & Bradway, P.W. (1987). *It happens to boys too.* Rape Crisis Center of Berkshire County, Inc., 18 Charles Street, Pittsfield, MA 01201.

Sgroi, S.M. (1982). *Handbook of clinical interventions in child sexual abuse.* Lexington, MA: Lexington Books.

Storm, K.A. (1986, April). Taped interview by F.H. Knopp.

Survivor: A Creative Journal by Men and Women Survivors of Sexual Assault. Redbaux Communications, 3636 Taliluna, Suite 125, Knoxville, TN 37919. Sample copy free.

Thomas, T. (1990). *Surviving with serenity: Daily meditations for incest survivors.* Health Communications, 3201 S.W. 15th Street, Deerfield Beach, FL 33442.

Thomas, T. (1989). *Men surviving incest: A male survivor shares the process of recovery.* Walnut Creek, CA: Launch Press.

Westerlund, E. (1987). *Incest: What to think, what to say, what to do.* Incest Resources, Inc., 46 Pleasant Street, Cambridge, MA 02139.

White, E.C. (1985). *Chain, chain, change.* Seattle, WA: Seal Press.

Appendix B

National Resources

Adults Molested as Children United, c/o The Giaretto Institute, 232 E. Gish Road, 1st Floor, San Jose, CA 95112 (408) 453-7616. Groups for women and men survivors and nationwide referrals.

Child Help National Child Abuse Hotline, P.O. Box 630, Hollywood, CA 90028 (1-800-422-4453). Crisis counseling and nationwide referrals for women and men survivors.

Incest Recovery Association, 6200 North Central Expressway, Suite 209, Dallas, TX 75206 (214) 373-6607. Therapy groups for women and men survivors, educational programs, materials, and newsletter.

Incest Survivor Information Exchange (I.S.I.E.), P.O. Box 3399, New Haven, CT 06515. Newsletter for women and men survivors to publish writings, art work, and exchange information.

Incest Survivors Resource Network International (ISRNI), P.O. Box 7375, Las Cruces, NM 88006 (505) 521-4260. Educational resources.

M.A.L.E., P.O. Box 380181, Denver, CO 80238-1181 (1-800-949-6253). Publishes *Men's Issues Forum,* a newsletter for male survivors.

Moving Forward, P.O. Box 4426, Arlington, VA 22204 (703) 271-4024. Bimonthly newsletter "for survivors of sexual child abuse and those who care for them." Writings by survivors and treatment professionals, national resources, conference calendar.

National Organization for Victim Assistance (NOVA), 1757 Park Road NW, Washington, DC 20004 (202) 232-NOVA. 24-hour service for information about local victim assistance groups.

Survivors Healing Center, P.O. Box 8491, Santa Cruz, CA 95061. For workshops and groups (408) 476-7174; for national referrals for women and men survivors (408) 427-0182.

Survivors of Incest Anonymous (SIA), P.O. Box 21817, Baltimore, MD 21222-6817 (301) 282-3400. Self-help groups for women and men survivors based on a 12-step program and educational materials.

Survivors Newsletter Collective, c/o Women's Center, 466 Pleasant Street, Cambridge, MA 02139. Volunteer collective of adult women survivors and quarterly newsletter.

Voices in Action, Inc., P.O. Box 148309, Chicago, IL 60614 (1-800-786-4238). National network of incest survivors and supporters of survivors, referrals, resource materials, conferences, and newsletter.

Appendix C

Choosing a Therapist for Child Sexual Abuse Issues*

With all the choices of therapists in your comunity, finding the right one for you or your child can be very difficult. Not all therapists are qualified in the area of child sexual abuse. It is up to you to interview potential therapists and make a careful decision. You, as an individual and a consumer, should obtain information about your therapist's qualifications, therapeutic background, and treatment philosophy.

In choosing the right therapist, it is important to consider your own values, attitudes, and feelings. Therapists may be from various disciplines: social work, psychology, counseling, psychiatry, or other associated fields. Each will approach therapy and the treatment of sexual abuse issues based on their own unique blend of experience, training, theoretical orientation, and individual personality.

The following gives you information about how to get started in finding a therapist and also provides a list of questions to ask. This list is not intended to cover every question you might have. You may want to add your own questions to the list provided, and you should not feel bound to ask all of these questions.

Developing a List of Therapists

The first thing you could do to start your search is to narrow your choices to two or three. If you have no idea who to call, look through the telephone yellow pages under the following headings: "Social Workers," "Psychologists," "Psychiatrists," "Marriage and Family Counselors," "Psychotherapists," or any other mental health-related field. See if anyone lists sexual abuse as their specialty.

Or, contact one of your social service or mental health agencies and request the names of competent sexual abuse therapists.

If transportation is a problem, you may need to narrow your search to a specific geographical area.

When you call therapists, tell them that you are in the process of choosing a therapist to help with your particular problem. Inform them that you have a number of questions that will take some time to answer. Ask if they are willing to answer the questions and whether a fee will be charged for that time. You may be able to do some preliminary screening if the therapist is willing to answer some of the questions over the phone.

Review the check list and be familiar with the questions before you see any of the therapists. If you have been referred to a particular therapist, review the

---

* Reproduced with permission of Carlos Loredo, PhD, Austin, Texas

checklist anyway. You might want to write the answers on a separate piece of paper if you contact more than one therapist. It would be helpful to make appointments with at least two therapists so you can compare their responses. Be aware that most therapists will ask you for information pertaining to the sexual abuse and your particular needs and expectations, so be prepared to answer some questions yourself.

Interviewing the Therapists

Experience and training:
— What academic degrees and/or other recognition or general training and experience do you have?
— Are you licensed or certified by a board? Which one?
— How many years of experience in providing therapy have you had?
— What internships or special training in sexual abuse have you had? Where and when? How long?
— Have you attended or conducted any sexual abuse workshops? If so, when and where?
— How many sexual abuse cases have you treated per year? How many are you currently treating?
— Do you specialize in any area of sexual abuse?
— Have you provided testimony in a court of law as a sexual abuse "expert"? How many times?
— How much experience have you had working with gays/lesbians? What is your philosophy about homosexuality?
— Do you deal with anything other than sexual abuse in your practice? What types of cases?
— Do you have supervision/consultation available to you?
— What kinds of clients do you typically see?
  Offender/victim
  Adults/children/teenagers
  Men/women
  Incest/rape
  Sexual innuendo (sexual harassment, etc.)
  Other
  What is the age range of children you serve?
  What is the age preference for your clients?

Familiarity and relationship with the community:
Ask the therapists what kind of community contact they have. Feel free to contact community agencies or other resources to see if they have heard of the therapist, or have any information to give you about them.

Ask the therapists to provide three references in the community (or other locale where she or he has practiced) of persons you can contact who are familiar with their work in sexual abuse.

Ask the therapists if a complaint has ever been filed against them, or with their certification/licensing board. If so, why, and what was the outcome?

Fees:

You have the right to ask these questions of the therapist—they are extremely important to your therapy.

— How much is your fee?
— Do you have a sliding fee scale? If so, what is the range?
— What are your billing and payment policies?
— Do you accept third-party (insurance) payments?
— Do you accept Victim Compensation payments?
— Do you accept alternate forms of payment (bartering, monthly payments)?
— Do you charge for a cancellation or "no show"?
— Do you charge for telephone consultations?
— What are your fees for the services offered?
   Evaluation reports:
   Expert testimony:
   Consultation:
   Testing:
   Type of treatment:
   Court preparation:
   Billing-related:
   Other:
— Are any of the items negotiable?

Treatment issues:

— Basically you will need to know from the therapist:
   What are we going to do?
   How are we going to do it?
   How long will it take?
   What do we hope to accomplish?
   How will we know when we've accomplished it?
— Are there any eligibility requirements, or type of cases you will not take?
— What are your typical working hours? Weekends? Evenings? Do you provide crisis intervention?
— How many other cases like mine have you treated?
— Do you maintain written progress notes? Will I have access to those notes?
— Will you provide written reports and progress summaries?

— What is your policy regarding confidentiality?

— How often, for how long, and with whom will you meet?

— Do you ever leave your office to provide services (for instance, home or school visits)?

— Would you report your clients if they physically or sexually abused children? (The correct answer is "yes.")

— Will you testify in court, if necessary? If so, are you willing to state a clear opinion and make specific recommendations?

Making the Decision

After each interview, make notes as soon as possible about your impressions of the therapist; if you interview more than one therapist, you may forget. In making the decision, consider these issues:

— How did the therapists respond to your questions and your needs?

— What was your reaction to the therapists?

> • Consider your own personal biases, values, and attitudes (religious preference, culture/ethnicity, feminist philosophy, role of advocacy, sexual preference, views regarding homosexuality).
>
> • Consider your special needs (for example, if you have problems with alcohol, drug abuse, or violence, etc., the therapist should be experienced in those areas).

— How did this therapist compare with the other(s) you interviewed?

Note: If your health plan does not provide coverage for a specialist in this area, you have the right to demand the care you need.

Special Consideration for Children

In addition to the questions already listed, you should ask the following if you are choosing a therapist for your child:

— What education/expertise do you have in child development?

— What is the extent of your experience in family therapy?

— Will you answer my questions and concerns about my child's behavior and help me understand and deal with it?

After You Have Been in Therapy Several Weeks, Consider How You Feel About Your Therapist:

— Are you intimidated by your therapist?

— Does your therapist listen to you?

— Do you feel you can disagree with your therapist?

— How does your therapist handle crisis and conflict?

At no point are you "stuck" with a particular therapist. If your own particular needs are not being met, you have the right to find another therapist more suitable to you. It is a good idea, however, to discuss your dissatisfaction with your therapist before terminating therapy.

Unfortunately, there are therapists who act sexually suggestive or otherwise victimize clients. If this happens to you, immediately report the therapist to his/her board and find another therapist.

Other Safer Society Publications

When Children Molest Children: Group Treatment Strategies for Young Sexual Abusers by C. Cunningham and K. MacFarlane, 1991, 240 pages, $28.00 including postage & handling

The Use of Victim-Offender Communication in the Treatment of Sexual Abuse: Three Intervention Models edited by J. Yokley, with Chapters by W. Bera, J. Hindman, L. Hutchens, D. McGuire, & J. Yokley, 1990, 112 pages, $17.50 including postage & handling

Female Sexual Offenders: An Exploratory Study by R. Mathews, J.K. Matthews, and K. Speltz, 1989, 112 pages, $17.50 including postage & handling

Fuel on the Fire: An Inquiry into "Pornography" and Sexual Aggression in a Free Society by J. Rosenberg, 1989, 96 pages, $13.95 including postage & handling

Treating the Young Male Victim of Sexual Assault: Issues & Intervention Strategies by E. Porter, 1986, 96 pages, $12.50 including postage & handling

Safer Society Press
Shoreham Depot Road, RR 1, Box 24-B, Orwell, Vermont 05760-9756
(802) 897-7541

All orders prepaid • Vermont residents please add sales tax

The Safer Society Program, a national project of the New York State Council of Churches, maintains nationwide lists of agencies, institutions, and individuals providing specialized assessment and treatment for youthful and adult sexual victims and offenders. It publishes papers, surveys, and pamphlets on these programs as well as on prevention issues, and networks among professionals serving victim and offender populations.

The Safer Society Program
Shoreham Depot Road, RR 1, Box 24-B, Orwell, Vermont 05760-9756
(802) 897-7541